Arto der Haroutunian is Armenian and was born in Aleppo, Syria. In the early fifties his father, who was a priest of the Armenian Apostolic Church, was invited to head the local church in Manchester and brought the family over to settle in England. Arto der Haroutunian qualified at Manchester University as an architect and set up his own practice.

In 1970, with his brother, they set up their first Armenian restaurant specializing in authentic Middle Eastern dishes. He has always been interested in good food and was fortunate enough to have an excellent teacher – his mother, whose advice and guidance was always sought over the preparing of menus for the restaurants.

Apart from catering and architecture, his main interest is painting, with which he has achieved a considerable degree of success. He has exhibited all over the world with works in many major collections. He is married with a young son.

D1016555

Arto der Haroutunian

Complete Arab Cookery

PANTHER
Granada Publishing

Panther Books
Granada Publishing Ltd
8 Grafton Street, London W1X 3LA

Published by Panther Books 1982
Reprinted 1985

A Granada Paperback UK Original

Copyright © Arto der Haroutunian 1982

ISBN 0-583-13559-5

Printed and bound in Great Britain by
Cox & Wyman Ltd, Reading
Set in Times

Contents

Acknowledgements
I would like to thank the following authors and publishers for their kind permission to use extracts from their books.

A Short History of the Arab People by J B Glubb, Hodder and Stoughton
Arabs in History by B Lewis, Hutchinson and Co
A Social and Economic History of the Near East in the Middle Ages by E Ashtor, Collins
In Aleppo Once by Altounyan, John Murray
Makers of Arab History by P Hitti, Macmillan

Note
Both Imperial and metric weights and measures are given in this book. Either should give perfect results but they are *not* equivalents and therefore are not interchangeable. Do not mix Imperial and metric weights and measures in the same recipe. Use either one or the other.

Introduction

'The combination of a tribal solidarity and a religious drive is overwhelming.'

Ibn Khaldoon, thirteenth-century historian

History and People

The history of the Arabs is a long one, and the Bedouins of the Arabian Peninsula, who have to date retained the tribal and nomadic customs of their ancestors, represent a way of life which goes back to prehistoric times. Yet exactly how far the Arabs go back, and whence they originated have still not been satisfactorily explained. The name Arab was first used to designate the nomadic tribes of Arabia, and it is still used in that sense; also the collective name in Arabic for a group of tents is an 'Aarab'. The origin of the word itself is obscure, it first being applied by the Mesopotamians to the people who dwelt to the west of the Euphrates valley.[1]

The ancient history of Arabia is not clear cut and too complex to discuss here, though it is worth noting that men of Semitic stock inherited and developed the great ancient empires of Assyria, Babylonia, Phoenicia and Southern Arabia.[2] In historical times wave upon wave of Arabians have come up from Southern and Central Arabia and found their way into the settled lands of the fertile crescent, urged on by poverty and hunger, where they began to cultivate the land. They still kept in touch with their kith in the oases, but gradually adopted the habits and customs of city dwellers.

In the seventh century AD these nomadic tribes established a great empire extending from Spain to the borders of China, and for nearly four centuries the Muslim inhabitants were known as Arabs; but with the disintegration of the empire, the people resumed their previous designations: Egyptians, Syrians, Iraqis, Persians etc.

To date there are over twenty countries or states that regard themselves as 'Arab'; but how Arab are they? Anthropologists and archaeologists have over the last few decades made extensive studies of the inhabitants of these 'Arab' lands, having recorded such physical characteristics as head shapes, height, skin, eyes, hair etc., revealing an extraordinary diversity of races.[3]

Since our prime interest is food we need not delve too deeply into the origins of the Arabs themselves; suffice it to say that for several thousands of years before either the name 'Arab' or the Arab people appeared in the annals of recorded history the inhabitants of the Middle East (Egypt, Iraq, Syria, Palestine) were not related racially to the Arabs. The Sumerians – 3000 BC – came from the east and settled in Iraq and northern Syria. The Hurrians, Hittites and Urartians came from the north, from the direction of Persia and Asia Minor; these races were Aryans. Syria, Lebanon, Palestine and Egypt were closely connected with, and colonized by, the Greeks and Romans, Iraq by Persians and Turks who in small numbers were scattered all over the Arab lands but especially in Egypt; Armenians settled in Syria, Lebanon and Northern Iraq; and Europeans – during the Crusades and after – on the entire coastline of the Eastern Mediterranean. 'The early Arab historians were aware of the racial diversities of their empire. They referred quite correctly to the tribes of Arabia as Arabs and to the subjects of their empires as Arabicized.'[4]

An unbelievable number of races have over the centuries found their way into this vast and arid land, the more significant ones being the Sumerians, Assyrians, Persians, Medes, Armenians, Kurds, Arabians and Mongolian-Turks, with a noticeable sprinkling of people from the Indian subcontinent, especially in the Gulf regions of the Arabian islands.

Thus the people of these lands share the same language today, but are still of many diverse races and origins. Let us attempt – albeit briefly – to make a broad analysis of these differences in character and origin.

Arabians

The majority of these people are today citizens of Saudi Arabia, but they are also found in the north in the desert area between Syria and the Euphrates, as well as in Southern Jordan.

The Arabians are the original Arabs. They have uniform characteristics and physically, mentally, and spiritually they resemble one another. There are very minor deviations and these one can trace in the Gulf regions where Persian and Indian blood have been mixed over the centuries. They are a practical, realistic people, being hardy individuals who over the ages have had to fight the desert for a meagre living.

The deserts of Arabia have never attracted foreign armies, and with certain exceptions – notably the holy cities of Mecca and Medina, where over the centuries other Muslims have established themselves – the whole vastness of Arabia throughout the ages, as today, has been sparsely populated.

When the Arabians broke out of their deserts and conquered their immense empire, they did so with armies of fifteen or twenty thousand men. It has been estimated that, when all the conquests were over, the Arabians represented only one per cent of the population of their empire. The remainder were a medley of many different races. Even today Arabian blood may well constitute only one or two per cent of that of the people of some of the Arab countries.[5]

The Southern Arabians – Yemenites – are most probably of a different origin to the Arabians, and probably have a fair amount of African and Indian blood.

Egyptians

By and large these people are the descendants of the Pharaohs, with a large mixture of Greek, Roman and especially Negroid African blood. From prehistoric times people from the south of the Sahara have passed through the Nile valley up to Egpyt and Libya. The river Nile has not only been the single source of Egypt's fertility but also the only passageway by which the Africans have passed.

The Egyptian people are in general easy-going, happy people; they are also submissive to authority and for thousands of years have been ruled by foreigners. They are slow and the rich Nile delta has over the generations made them inactive and indolent.

It is not the southern sun, as Montesquieu imagines, but the luxuriance of southern soil and the abundance of provisions that relax the exertions of the inhabitants and cause apathy. When a man is almost certain of finding sufficient food, however coarse or simple, he is easily tempted to indulge in laziness. By the fertility of Egypt, Mesopotamia and India, which yield their produce almost spontaneously, the people are lulled into indolence; while in neighbouring countries, of a temperature equally warm, as among the mountains of Yemen and Syria where hard labour is necessary to ensure a good harvest, we find a race as superior in industry to the former as the inhabitants of North Europe are to those of Spain and Italy.[6]

When Burkhardt wrote the foregoing lines in the early part of the nineteenth century he was not very aware of, nor would have much cared about, the fact that not only the lands of the people he described were different, but that the people themselves were ethnically different.

Syrians
Here we should temporarily forsake political boundaries, since for all purposes the modern Lebanese and Palestinians are historically Syrians, having had the same past and racial origins.

The history of Syria is one long string of foreign invasions. From the dawn of history an endless succession of invading armies and migrating tribes, races and ideas travelled up and down the narrow-shaped strip which was the coastline of this part of the Mediterranean. This crescent is where literally everything has happened throughout the ages. It was here that the three great religions – Judaism, Christianity and Islam – were born. It was here where some of the oldest known cultures and civilizations were developed; the world for thousands of years evolved around these coastlines and spread out only slowly in other directions. Syria throughout the ages was in the centre of this evolution. The recently discovered ruins of Ebla,[7] which stretch our knowledge of the area well beyond biblical dates, portrays a rich, advanced culture well equipped with all the necessities of an organized society. In 539 BC the Persians conquered Syria; then came Alexander the Great in 333 BC; thereafter for a thousand years Syria remained under Greek and Roman rule.

Thus the people of Syria are formed from a mixture of Greek, Roman, Hittite, Hurrian, Philistine, Armenian and Kurdish races. In the words of J. B. Glubb: 'The Syrians are racially unrelated to the Arabs of Arabia. Many of their characteristics resemble those of the Greeks, particularly their extreme intellectual subtlety . . . They are socially charming, extremely courteous and the heirs of thousands of years of culture.'[8]

Iraqis
These people are less intellectual, less polite and courteous than the Syrians – 'but are a stronger and coarser strain'.[9]

In the year AD 570, on 20 August, a child was born in Mecca (Arabia) who was to transform history. His name was Muhammed. He was orphaned early in life, being brought up by his grandfather and later by his uncle. He married a rich widow and was a man who loved solitude and meditation, who was quiet, kindly and affectionate. One night in the year 610, when he was 40 years old, he was visited by the Archangel Gabriel.

> Read in the name of the Lord who created,
> Who created of man of blood coagulated,

Read! the Lord is the most beneficent,
Who taught by the pen,
Taught what they knew not to men.

Muhammed, in fear and trepidation, ran from his cave to throw himself over a precipice, at which moment he saw the Archangel Gabriel 'in the form of a man with his feet astride the horizon'.[10] Bewildered, he ran home to confide his visions to his wife, Khadija, who unwaveringly declared her belief that he was the prophet of the Arabs.

Soon Muhammed was preaching his message. His teaching was simple – God was one and idols were to be destroyed. He was the apostle of God. One day the dead would rise again, the righteous would receive eternal happiness, the idolators only hell-fire. After several setbacks, frustrations and tribal wars, Muhammed succeeded in persuading the great majority of the 'Arab' tribes to accept him as the messenger of God and thus he achieved his other aim of uniting all the nomadic tribes plus the sedentary tribes into one. 'And if Allah pleases, He would make you a simple nation.'[11]

On 8 June in the year 632, the prophet died after a short illness. He had achieved a great deal. He had brought a new religion to the pagan people of Arabia. He had provided them with the sacred book, the Koran, which contained the uncreated and eternal truth as revealed to him by the Angel Gabriel. He had established a well organized and armed state.

His death was followed at first by internal disunity and struggle but gradually under the leadership of Khalif Abu Bekr the Muslim Arabs overran the whole of Syria and Iraq, defeating the Byzantine and Persian forces. They then marched against Egypt and after some initial difficulties they negotiated with Cyrus, the governor of Babylon (not to be confused with the ancient Kingdom in Iraq), and Commander Amr ibn al Assi,[12] in the name of Allah, entered Egypt in triumph.

The ruling Khalif at this time was Umar ibn al Khattab. In his ten years of rule the Arabs conquered an empire, yet he had remained pious, simple and compassionate. A truly great ruler, he was assassinated by a Persian slave while praying in a mosque.

After Umar's death, and especially after the murder of the next Khalif – Othman, the Arab world changed dramatically; all the desert instincts of murder, selfishness and hatred reappeared whilst the pious Muslim's dream of God having chosen his race to conquer and rule the world and with promises of the wonder of paradise to come, evaporated into the desert dunes. What followed can only be described as the near-disintegration of all that the prophet had tried to build. For six years inter-family, inter-tribal murders and manoeuvrings took place until Muawiya in AD 661 assumed the role of Khalif. Thus began the Umaiyid Khalifate (661–750) which was based in Damascus and featured once again much in-fighting, bloodshed and eventual civil war. It was followed by the Abbasid Khalifate (750–861).

The Umaiyids, having conquered most of the lands which in time were amalgamated into the empire, left the Abbasids only the job of consolidation and 'settling down'. The first Abbasid Khalif, Saffan, was followed by one of the most energetic Arab rulers – Khalif Mansoor, who planned and built the new capital of Baghdad on what was then Persian land; the centre of power had now moved from the Mediterranean to Mesopotamia; from its Byzantine and Roman past to a more truly Eastern venue, that of Persia.

The Abbasids, following centuries-old Asian traditions, surrounded themselves with the pomp and ceremony of an elaborate and hierarchic court. The influence of the old Persian order of the Sassanids became overwhelming. The administration was no longer based on religious discrimination and racial exclusiveness. The Khalifs made more and more use of their freed men, placing them in important positions of government; thus Greeks, Turks, Armenians and Berbers received new powers and opportunities for self-aggrandizement.

The greatest Abbasid Khalif was Haroun al Rasheed who was loved by his people and whose name and fame have become legends in Arabic literature. Poets praised him, scholars admired him, and even his bitterest foes – the Byzantines – begrudgingly accepted his greatness. He was a tall handsome man – open, honest, a great lover of poetry and music, always anxious for intellectual self-improvement. During the period AD 786–806 the life of the empire had reached the stage where conquest, wealth and commercialism were passing to intellectualism. Haroun al Rasheed appointed a Syrian Christian to translate into Arabic the medical works of the ancients from Latin, Greek and Syriac. Many other scholars (mostly captured Christian or Persian slaves) laboured in translating geographical, mathematical and historic texts.

The influx of foreigners soon made Baghdad a cosmopolitan city, with Greeks, Armenians and Jews having their own quarters. The palaces of the rich contained servants of many races – all captured during numerous expeditions against other lands.

Yet in Baghdad there was freedom of religion; though the state religion was Islam, others were tolerated, and indeed until the tenth and eleventh centuries a fair proportion of the populace was still Christian; there were also some Jews and Magians (members of the old religion of Persia). In time most of these people were converted to Islam.

Haroun al Rasheed died at the age of 47 in AD 809. His death brought tension and strife between his two sons Muhammed al Amin and Abdulla al Mamoon. With the former's murder in AD 813 the Khalifate went to Mamoon who proved to be a worthy successor to his father al Rasheed.

Al Mamoon's capital soon rose to eminence as a commercial, industrial and intellectual centre . . . but the glory of Al Mamoon's age did not lie solely in such fields. It lay in the impetus the Khalif gave to learning and to intellectual activity. The movement developed into one of the most momentous in Islam if not in the history of thought.[13]

Yet triumphs of the intellect were counterbalanced by a rapid disintegration of the empire. With the loss of Khurasan to Tahir the Ambidextrous who established his own dynasty, Mamoon (as his father did before) turned to the Turkish tribes living on the steppes of Central Asia for manpower. The years from 833 until 975 saw the crumbling of the empire; a gradual decline that culminated in the virtual extinction of the Khalifate and its replacement by puppet Khalifs who were chosen, dismissed or murdered at the will of the Turkish soldiers who had initially been brought in as slaves or mercenaries to protect the empire from the steppelands of Asia and the Caucasus.[14] In the year 861 the same Turkish mercenaries assassinated the then Khalif, Mutawakkil, and the glory of the empire came to a virtual end.

The Arab Empire had lasted some 250 years; henceforth the power balance in the Middle East shifted. From the west the Byzantines – reinforced and reinvigorated – moved down to Syria where also many independent Muslim principalities were created. Then came the Seljuqs under Tughril Beq and Alp Arslan who plundered and ravaged their way through Persia and Armenia and began to destroy the very foundations of both the Arab and the Byzantine Empires. The Seljuqs were followed by the Mongols who, in turn, laid waste to whatever there was left to lay waste to!

In 1095, Pope Urban II preached the first Crusade and suddenly after several centuries the Middle East was once again a battleground between East and West. After a few initial successes the Christian evangelist-plunderers gradually lost their footholds in the Orient, leaving behind pockets of Christian enclaves that survive to this day. The Mamlooks from Egypt together with the Mongols from Asia under Genghis Khan yet again devastated the Arab lands.

This story of conquest, devastation and plunder culminated in the destruction of Baghdad on 18 January 1258 by the forces of Hulagu. The Khalif, Mutasim, gave himself up and Hulagu ordered him to instruct the whole civil population to gather on the plain outside the city walls, where they all were shot, or slashed and hacked to death.

After Baghdad it was the turn of Damascus (sacked by Tamerlane and burnt to the ground) then Aleppo in the north was sacked. Finally there was nothing left of the Syria of the Umaiyids.

This constant warring of the Mongol tribes culminated in the ascendance of the tribe of Othman (1288–1326) whose heirs slowly – but much in the same spirit of their fellow Mongols – conquered Syria, Palestine and Egypt. In the East the Persians under the Safavids incorporated the whole of Iraq, only shortly to lose it to the Mamlooks (who were of Christian birth, forcibly converted to Islam, trained initially to fight for the Khalifs but in time for themselves).

The Ottoman Empire thus ruled (or, according to opinion, misruled) the entire Middle East until the aftermath of the First World War. In his masterpiece *The Seven Pillars of Wisdom*, T. E. Lawrence sums up the Ottoman rule in the following words:

Early in the Middle Ages the Turks found a footing in the Arab States, first as servants, then as helpers and then as a parasite growth which choked the life out of the old body politic . . . by stages Semite Asia passed under their yoke, and found it a slow death. Their goods were stripped from them . . . Turkish rule was gendarme rule and Turkish political theory as crude as its practice . . . even the Arabic language was banished from the courts and offices . . . the Arabs would not give up their rich and flexible tongue for crude Turkish; instead, they filled Turkish with Arabic words.[15]

The Arabs, who on many occasions had risen against their barbarian overlords, took up arms in 1917 and the news of the Hejaz Rising resulted in the spread of anti-Turkish feeling in Syria and Lebanon.

The British took Damascus in 1918 and set up an Arab government under Ameer Faisal. The French landed in Lebanon then immediately seized Syria; in effect they controlled that area until 1945 when both countries became independent. Iraq fell under the British sphere of influence, while Egypt since 1882 was already under British control.

After the Second World War Syria, Lebanon, Jordan, Iraq, Saudi Arabia and Egypt regained their independence and are today, together with the United Arab Emirates, North and South Yemen, members of the United Nations and sovereign states of varying colours, each in a different stage of social and political development. They are all trying to make up for centuries of deprivation from the sphere of body politics and are endeavouring to update their societies.

The wheel has turned full circle once more. After a thousand years the 'Arab' states have now once again regained their individual independence and although they still retain the Islamic faith and the Arabic language which act as a common link, they will in the centuries to come move on towards their very own national directions – paths which at the end of all arguments are based more on geographical and ethnic considerations rather than on superficial and easily replaceable codes of conduct and modes of speech.

Finally, in the words of the poet – a feeling shared by all Arabs who lament those centuries which are now only memories and spectres on their soils:

I weep for a land fashioned to beauty fair,
Beyond compare;
I weep for a heritage of glory and fame,
A hard, far aim.
I weep for spirits too indolent to urge men,
To battle again;
I weep for the splendour of empire and the boast.
Turned all to a ghost.

Khair-el-din-Ziri Kli

Food in History

The basis of society in Arabia, especially in the south, was agriculture. Cereals, myrrh, incense, aromatics and spices were extensively produced and exported, the latter being famous throughout the world. The caravan routes passed through Arabia; from Syria through Arabia to the Yemen where the Indian vessels came to the Yemenite ports bringing spices, fruits and the basic Arab food, rice. Textiles, food, wine and most probably the art of writing reached the Arabs from the north via Anatolia and Syria.

The basic diet of the Arabian comprised (and still comprises) dates, rice, milk, goat's or lamb's meat and coffee. Great must have been the joy of those early Arabs who with hunger in their bellies and Islam in their hearts, marched to conquer in the name of Allah those rich, green lands the prophet had promised to them.

We have poured down water in showers,
We have broken up the earth in cracks,
And have caused to sprout in grain,
And vines and green shoots,
Olives and palms,
And orchards luxuriant,
Fruit trees and pastures,
For you and your flocks to enjoy.

Koran LXXX

For compared to their vast barren homes the fertile valleys
and hills of Syria, Egypt, Iraq and Iran must have appeared
like the promised paradise of the Koran:

And for him who fears to stand before his Lord are two gardens
  full of varieties –
Therein are two fountains flowing!
Therein are pairs of every fruit.
Reclining on beds, whose inner coverings are of silk brocade,
And the fruits of the two gardens are within reach . . .
Therein are fruits, palms and pomegranates,
Therein are goodly beautiful ones,
Pure ones confined to pavilions,
Before them man has not touched them nor jinni,
Reclining on green cushions and beautiful carpets . . .

Koran Ar – Rahman

And indeed, the lush valleys of Syria, with her millennia of
history, commerce and culture, with the rich dark earth of
the Nile delta where man reaped all the goodness that nature
provides, was the paradise the Arab was seeking.

Paradise was regained in the name of Allah! with the
sword; and the land was irrigated with innocent blood. The
Arab

. . . turned the mill-wheels of Jalula with the blood of his
enemies . . . When all the Christians heard the shouts of the
Saracens crying 'Allah Akbar', they were amazed and confounded,
imagining that the whole Saracen army had come from
Damascus . . . for the spoils. They seized all the silks, cloths,
household stuff, fruits and provisions that were in the fair and all
the hangings, money and plate in the monastery . . . so they loaded
all their jewels, wealth and furniture upon horses, mules and asses
and returned to Damascus, having left nothing behind them
(having killed 10,000 people) but the old monks . . .[16]

The Arab

. . . who rode upon a red camel with a couple of sacks, in one of which he carried that sort of provision which the Arabs call sawik, which is either barley, rice or wheat, sodden and unhusken; the other was full of fruits. Before him he carried a very great leather bottle . . . behind him a large wooden platter.[17]

soon acquired all the fineness and sophistications of the conquered races. From the Egyptians he took such age-old recipes as El Ful, Melokhia, Ta'Amia, Bamia and many others, all tried and tested since the days of the Pharaohs. From the Syrians he adopted many olive-oil-based dishes especially salads of cucumber, leek, onions, cos lettuce, while bananas and oranges came from the Lebanese. From Assyria (Iraq) came the abundance of dates, hazelnuts, mushrooms, cherries and figs; from Armenia and Kurdistan the cereal burghul (cracked wheat), pomegranates and water melon from the region of Van; sesame oil and tahina from Cilicia and Cappadocia. From the Caucasus came many varieties of kebabs and from the Assyrian Armenian cuisine the classic stuffed vegetable dishes (mahshi) such as Sheik-el Mahshi, or Betingan Mahshi; and from the Persians came 'Persian milk-yogourt', also the art of cooking rice and vegetables together, various sweet 'sherbets', drinks and especially the ingenious method of creating sweet and sour dishes. The foods of the conquered people formed the basis of the present Arab culture.

From these rich backgrounds over the ages, the Arabs – who gradually ceased to be a pure race but more a commonwealth of differing people with the same religion and, in time, language – enriched their cuisine by either straight adaptation or Arabicization of the social habits and customs of the conquered races. This transformation was not achieved overnight but through calculated and methodical subjugation, since the conqueror had the sword, the faith and the language.

Faith comes from the divine law which is written in the language of the Arabs because the prophet himself was an Arab – hence all other languages were banned in the Muslim dominions and thus we find Omar, forbidding the use of the jargon of foreigners and calling their speech Khibb (fraud and deception) – Arabic became the language of the administration of the Muslim Empire, all the other languages were abandoned . . . Arabic became their language . . .[18]

Names, buildings, languages, morals, customs and religions were changed as everything was Arabicized. Yet, people's names and habits may change but their food and music never! So what the 'Arab' people eat today is very much the same as the people ate in the Middle East before Islam; understandably much developed and enriched with the process of time and with the introduction and addition of new spices and vegetables such as tomatoes, potatoes etc. For the greatest asset of Arabic cooking is in its traditionalism, its adherence to the past, the unwavering, almost singular attachment to 'one's grandmother's recipe', which enables us to appreciate and often trace the origin of a particular mode of cooking or recipe.

Perhaps until the ninth century the Arabs, who were still a minority among their conquered races, still ate their 'dates, rice and milk' but henceforth in the 'City of Haroun al Rasheed, Baghdad, with ancient glories bright' they began to acquire a habit of luxury which neither the desert nor their grandfathers, who had ridden with sacks and bottles and wooden platters, had ever known.

The Abbasid Arabs, dazzled by the opulence and sophistication of the Iranians they had conquered, threw themselves wholeheartedly into adopting and imitating all that came their way. Baghdad, founded by Khalif Mansoor, grew rapidly. Fine houses filled the surrounding countryside. Fountains played in the courtyards and the walls of the houses were covered with brilliant colours. There were large bazaars all over the city, each bazaar specializing in one commodity, eg food and vegetables or meats or textiles. Each trade had its own street. People of all nations came to this fabulous city, this 'Bride of the World'. The input of foreigners made Baghdad a cosmopolitan city and most wealthy families employed cooks from different nations to enable them to enjoy varied types of cooking.

It was in this rich, opulent era of the 'Sons of Abbas' that perhaps the greatest heights of cooking were achieved. A period of Persian ascendancy took place in literature, in the arts and sciences, though a vast number of the populace lived in the poorest circumstances in surroundings similar to those which Pilts described in his *An Englishman in Mecca in 1687*: 'Thirty-seven days marching time and three days tarrying . . . in all this way there is scarce any green thing to be met with, nor beast nor fowl to be seen or heard; nothing but sand and stones.'

All over the empire slaves and the peasantry rose time after time in rebellion against arrogant, selfish and inhuman rule; yet in the palaces of the rich, especially those of the Khalifs, songs were sung about food, poems were written and manuals were composed on the noble arts of cooking and eating. Unfortunately very little has come down to us. To date only two manuscripts of recipes have been found: one is *Kitab al Wusha il al Habib*, from the thirteenth century; the other, written in 1226 in Baghdad by Muhammed al Baghdadi.[19] The recipes described and included in these manuscripts were those of the court and not of the masses, who continued to eat their traditional food. Maxim Rodinson, who has made a deep study of *Kitrab al Wusha il al Habib*, believes that the author was a Syrian because of the abundance of Syrian and especially North Syrian dishes, some still widely popular today. The author of the second manuscript was most probably of Persian extraction since it abounds with Iranian-inspired recipes.

Intermarriage and imitation caused the Arabs progressively to succumb to the strong influence of the autochthonous civilizations . . . which predominated in order of food, dress and furniture . . . the upper strata of Arab society were more inclined to take over the fashions of the old autochthonous civilizations.[20]

Thus the merchant classes, mostly Christians and Jews, did their utmost to satisfy the cravings of the aristocracy and from all corners of the empire and beyond brought to Baghdad the grains of Armenia, fruits from Damascus, 'the produce of which were highly appreciated in Iraq and Egypt'.[21]

The very rich ate off dishes of gold, set with precious stones. In hot weather ice was used for drinks and indeed Khalif Mehedi on his pilgrimage to the holy cities even transported ice on camels to cool his drinks. The ice was brought from the Iranian mountains, being wrapped in layers of sacking on which water was continually poured by specially trained slaves.

In the final days of the empire when rebellion was rife throughout the provinces and hosts of 'Turks and Tartars shake their swords at thee, meaning to mangle all their provinces',[22] decadence had set in. The élite classes indulged in luxury, self-contentment and in the belief of unhampered continuity. History however is out constantly to disprove 'continuity'. Thus the moon paled, the sun set and the glory was no more. There was pillage, destruction and mass annihilation of people by the Mongols, Mamlooks and Turks 'who are wholly deficient in virtue, honour and justice – and honesty is only to be found in their paupers or idiots',[23] together with the break-up of the basic structure of the empire, with one region after another declaring independence. Then as though ordained by Allah – at the sight of all this debauchery and ungodliness – came earthquakes, pestilence, plagues and famine, culminating in the impoverishment of what was left of the people, the almost total disappearance of the once flourishing industries and trades, and in the complete destruction of agriculture and the arable lands.

The golden age of the thousand and one great nights with their feasts, banquets and orgies became mere tales of the imagination as the people of the 'Arab' lands entered their second Dark Age, while rival powers fought for the few remaining palm trees and water wells.

> I can almost hear the palm trees drinking rain,
> In Iraq, the villagers groan and exiles,
> With oars and sails struggling against the gusts,
> And thunders of the Gulf, chanting:
> Rain, rain,
> Famine in Iraq.[24]

The next important culinary influence on Arabic cuisine was that of the Ottoman Empire. The origins of Ottoman cuisine were very similar to those of the Arabs. The Mongolian nomadic tribes had very little of their own – 'meat, kumiss (mare's milk), and a few dumplings in their sacks'.[25] They too, like the Arabs, succumbed to the strong influence of the autochthonous civilizations. They were soon converted to Islam, adopted the Arab's alphabet and augmented their meagre language with that of the Persians and Arabs. They naturally took a great interest in the social and cultural customs of these two Muslim peoples.

The important contribution of the Ottomans was that, having conquered several Christian lands – Byzantium, Armenia, Greece, Bulgaria and Hungary, they reintroduced into the world of Islam a great many pre-Arab customs, foods and manners. Thus thanks to the Ottomans, the Syrians, together with the Palestinians and the Egyptians, once again had access to their earlier culture. This fusion of Arabic-European, Islamic-Christian, with native Mongolian culture created in the ensuing centuries a new cuisine, that of the Ottomans.

It is therefore not surprising to find similar dishes appearing in several 'modern' countries, since all these countries were until some seventy to eighty years ago still part of an empire, the official language of which for the past five to six hundred years has been Turkish. It would take a very learned and brave person to commit himself to naming a particular recipe as being Arab or Turkish or otherwise without some reservations, yet certain social, regional, religious and climatic characteristics should in most instances help to clarify certain points.

Since the collapse of the Ottoman Empire and the emergence of the Middle Eastern states the food of the region has been gradually evolving. A certain internationalism with its bland monotony has also affected the cuisine of the Arabs. The Lebanese have, for a while now, opted for everything French; the people of Egypt, Iraq and the Gulf States have moved towards Americanized easy, quick services with 'petata-chap', 'creme-chap' and 'English custard', which easily outstrip all the traditional 'muhalebiyehs' in the Gulf States. Cornflakes are replacing yogourt and bread breakfasts while Horlicks has taken over from goat's milk and a strong cup of coffee.

In the luxury hotels and restaurants of Cairo, Damascus or Beirut one is offered what are aptly called 'international menus', but in the small back-street cafés and restaurants, some of the flavour of the East can still be captured. However, a number of these establishments unfortunately have gone the way of commercialism and just as one often meets in America and Europe such ribaldries as 'kebab houses' or 'hummus and falafel bars', so one can meet a 'falafel house' next to a 'Kentucky Fried Chicken' or 'Wimpy Bar' in the heart of Beirut or Amman.

This loss of tradition is equally augmented with the large exodus of the peasantry away from their villages to the cities, where under the constant bombardment of tinned, pre-packed convenience foods in a generation or two the traditional dishes and centuries-old recipes are forgotten or dismissed.

'Don't tell me you like Bamia. Why that's not fit enough even for our servants. Or Kubbeh. Dear me no. So much trouble, such a waste of time.' As the Kombar said to the Kyky, 'How sweet is a fig for breakfast.' 'Learn better manners, oh Kombar,' he replied. 'After bread nothing deserves notice.'[26]

So say some, nothing is better than the recipes of old, tested and tried over the centuries, but unfortunately 'where the stomach is concerned wisdom withdraws'.

Climatic, Social and Religious Influences

'Allah surely gives food to everyone but its quality and kind are dictated by what man deserves.'[27]

Over nearly the whole of south-western Asia, south of the mountain belt of Iran and Turkey, lie the 'Arab' lands. These are well defined on the north by a mountainous rim and demarcated on all other sides by the sea, except along the narrow isthmus of Suez which separates it from Africa. The dominant feature of the whole area is the great plateau of Arabia with its high south-western edge overlooking the Red Sea and its long, gentle slope north-eastwards to the plains of Iraq. In the east the plateau merges into the fold mountain country of Oman. In the west along the Mediterranean Sea are the north-to-south mountain-and-valley systems of Syria, Palestine and Jordan. Geologically the whole area, with the exception of the fold ranges of Oman, consists of an ancient block of metamorphic rocks.

The Tropic of Cancer passes through the heart of Arabia and across the centre of the Red Sea; the parallel of 3°N, which passes through the centre of the eastern Mediterranean, passes slightly to the north of Beirut, Damascus and Baghdad. The cyclones which bring rainfall to Mediterranean lands give Syria, Palestine and Jordan a characteristic winter rainfall as they work their way into the Mesopotamian plains.

The natural vegetation of most of south-western Asia is the evergreen Mediterranean woodlands, passing gradually into scrub and desert as the rainfall decreases. There are great differences in natural vegetation and cultivated crops. On the coastal plains of the Mediterranean the crops are oranges, bananas, corn and all kinds of vegetables. Beirut is known for olives, Tripoli for oranges and mandarins, Latakia for tobacco, while the mulberry trees of Northern Syria are famous. Liquorice root is found growing far and wide near marshes and river banks, while pistachios are often called 'Aleppo nuts'. Syria also produces good-quality barley, maize and wheat as does Iraq, where rice is grown along the river valleys as well as dates.

Dates are of course the staple food of not only the Iraqis and Arabians but of most desert people. They are utilized in a great variety of ways; syrup and vinegar are made from old dates; the terminal part of the date palm is eaten as a vegetable; the leaves of the palm tree are used for making matting and thatching houses; the fibre of the outer trunk for rope; the timber for building; and, finally, the famed oriental spirit arak is made from dates.

Egypt, of course, has the Nile and apart from slight winter rainfall along the Mediterranean coast the country is virtually rainless. Thus for centuries along the two banks of the Nile the Egyptian fellah has lived in a mud-brick house with hens for eggs and manure, a buffalo for pulling his plough and – if rich enough – a donkey for transport. His crops are wheat, clover and cotton.

The striking feature of Middle Eastern agriculture in the days of the Arab Empire was the predominance of wheat.

White bread was a household commodity, while only in the late Middle Ages did wheaten bread appear in Europe and then only amongst the upper classes. Rice, which had been planted in Iraq in the distant past, acquired a new popularity during the time of the Khalifs; this phenomenon can be easily explained, for the Persians, Mamlooks and Mongolian Turks were rice eaters and due to their mass immigration to Iraq rice slowly supplanted wheat. Also, some of the richest wheatlands of Egypt, Armenia and Syria were cut off from the rest of the empire, so that the people of the deserts as well as the empire relied more and more on rice. Today rice is still the staple diet of the Arabs and only in parts of Syria and Lebanon, primarily among Christians – ie Assyrians, Armenians, Maronites and some Kurds, does burghul (cracked wheat) still predominate.

The most striking feature of Arabic cooking is not the broad similarities found from one end of the region to the other but the discrepancies due to climatic, ethnic and social differences. The religion of Islam is the one unifying factor of the Arab people, the Koran its spokesman and guide.

The majority of Arabs still live in a village society with a reverent attachment to nature and with the village fountain as the source of community life. Certain trees are considered holy, eg the dire and the abbhar (whose nuts are used for making rosaries) while each grain of wheat bears upon it the single indentation or stroke of the Arabic letter *Alif* – the first letter of God's name. However, it is to the land that the peasants' emotions in the world of nature are most closely tied. For the land was there at the time of man's birth and will be there after his departure. Folk songs are filled with metaphors and similes expressed in terms of the natural and flowering world. The dry season is the busiest time in the peasant's year, for it is then that work begins in the vineyards and orchards. The family quarters are aired, the sheep-wool quilts and other household equipment are moved into the sunlight.

> Open the windows Spring is coming,
> From our orchards the wind is singing,
> Twining, twisting, twinkling her way,
> In our orchards Spring is blooming.[28]

With the coming of Spring the sheep are sheared – the wool being kept for stuffing quilts, for spinning by the older women, and for making sweaters and socks. August is the time of the grain harvest. During the busy weeks of reaping and threshing, all available village hands turn into the fields. Crops brought from the fields, gardens and orchards are converted into foodstores for winter consumption – the flat rooftops serving as sorting and drying areas. Here grain, lentils, beans and chickpeas are spread on goat-hair rugs, then sorted and sieved. Aubergines, courgettes, tomatoes, okra, figs etc are sliced open and laid in the heat of the sun for drying and preserving purposes. Figs, apricots and tomatoes are also converted into pastes by slow simmering in outdoor cauldrons over brush and dung fires.

Grapes are harvested in August and September. They are converted into winter stores, dried as raisins or made into bekmaz (thick treacle used as a spread on butter). The fat-tailed sheep are overfed and fattened, rafters are strengthened, stacks of dung cakes and faggots are piled against doors ready for use on the hearth. Food is sealed in bins and jars which are then stored in niches along the walls. Strings of onions and garlic hang from the rafters. Goat-hair rugs are spread on the floors.

Within doors a close community life flourishes. Stories are told of ancient days of valour and honour. The love of their ancestors is rekindled and transmitted to the young ones so that traditions may continue. Young girls are taught to cook and sew, old people turn to crafts, women to spinning and knitting.

The Koran guides the villages throughout the year, for the Koran advocates hospitality and chivalry – a great characteristic of the Arab people, even in the pre-Islamic times. Thus for thousands of years the manners and way of life of the people of Egypt, Syria, Lebanon, Iraq and Arabia in general have hardly changed.

In a Muslim house the front door leads to the reception room (used by men only), a separate door leading to the domestic apartments. Arabs entertain warmly and generously. The host sets before his guests, whoever they may be, all the food he has in his house. In the poor villages or in the tents of the nomads there will often be little furniture, and the guest room (or tent) will be spread with rugs or carpets, with mattresses, quilts and cushions laid round the walls for people to sit on.

When food is served it is brought either in one large dish or, more popularly, in small plates to be placed in the centre of the room. The guests are then invited to sit round and eat. Normally the guests eat alone but they may invite their host to join them. Often, however, the host refuses since he considers it his duty to wait upon his guests. Before and after food, a jug of water and a basin are brought round for the guests to wash their hands.

The Arabs believe that 'the first duty of a host is cheerfulness'; the guest in turn must 'guard his voice, shorten his sight and praise the food'.[29] The Koran advises to 'sow wheat and not thorns and all the people will like and love you' and 'do not enter other people's homes except with permission and good manners'. A guest must first refuse the food offered to him but after two or three such requests must give in. He must never refuse dishes which have been tasted by others as this gives offence.

'Bismillah' ('in the name of God') is repeated by all several times before the meal is started and 'Shukran Allah' ('thanks to God') when the meal is over. The Koran consists of the revelations which the prophet Muhammed received through the Angel Gabriel as messages from God and which he delivered to his followers who wrote them down. Muhammed deals lengthily with food and insists particularly on its beneficial character as a gift from God.

Oh man, eat the lawful and good things, from what is in the earth and follow not the footsteps of the devil . . . Forbidden to you is that which dies of itself, and blood and flesh of swine and that on which any other name than that of Allah has been invoked, and the strangled and the beaten to death and that killed by a fall, and that killed by the goring of a horn, and that which wild beasts have eaten – except what you slaughter, and that which is sacrificed on stones set up (for idols) and that you seek to divide by arrows, that is a transgression.

For those on pilgrimage the Koran advises 'Oh you who believe, kill not game while you are on pilgrimage.' For those on the sea: 'Lawful to you is the game of the sea and its food a provision to you and for the travellers.'

All fruits and vegetables are permitted. 'Then we cause to grow gardens of palm trees and grapes for you. You have therein many fruits and of them you eat, and a tree that grows out of Mount Sinai, which produces oil and relish for the eaters.' 'And surely there is a lesson for you in the cattle, we make you to drink of what is in their bellies, and you have in them many advantages and of them you eat.'

The Koran forbids all forms of alcoholic or fermented drinks. The Khalif Omar stressed later that these included any drink made from grapes, dates, wheat, barley and honey. When an animal is to be slaughtered, the person who is about to perform the execution has to say, 'In the name of Allah, Allah is most great.' Then the throat of the animal is cut. This meat is then regarded as 'hallal'.

Religious Festivals

Muslims are supposed to pray five times a day: before sunrise, at noon, in the afternoon, at sunset and at night.

The Muslim year differs by ten days from the calendar year, thus the Muslim months do not always come at the same season. In the month of Ramadan (ie the month in which the Koran was revealed) Muslims are forbidden to eat, drink, smoke and make love from first dawn to sunset. The Lesser feast comes at the end of Ramadan.[30] The Great feast falls on the 10th of the month of Dhuel Hijja, and is the day of pilgrimage outside Mecca. Both feast days are occasions of public holiday; children are dressed in new clothes and friends and relations call upon one another to exchange greetings. 'Eid Mubaarak' ('fortunate feast'), 'Allah Yubaarak Feet' ('may God make you and yours fortunate too').

People enter each other's homes, sit down and take sweets and coffee then leave after a suitable pause; children are often presented with small gifts. 'Those who keep their duty are indeed in a secure place – in gardens and springs. Wearing fine and thick silk, facing one another, thus shall it be, and we shall join them to pure beautiful ones.'

Characteristics of the Cuisine

> A crust of dry bread is enough for the wise,
> But a city's supplies of stuffed golden mutton,
> Cannot please the desires of a glutton.[31]

Lamb is the meat of the Arabs; there is very little beef and no pork. Whilst the Arabians generally either roast or more often boil their meat in lightly salted or spiced water with a little oil, the Syrians and the Kurds of Iraq prefer to grill or fry theirs.

Most Arab dishes are stews of one kind or another. A favourite method is to stew meat (cut into small portions) in milk or yogourt, accompanied with vegetables such as onions or garlic, and spices. The medieval manuscripts are full of dishes cooked in yogourt. Today cream is often substituted for milk or yogourt, especially in the Gulf States.

Arabic cuisine lacks the versatility of Armenian-Turkish grilled meats – kebabs, and indeed Arabic kebabs betray their origin from their names, eg 'Kebab Halibi', 'Kebab Ammani', or 'Shashlig' or 'Kebab Kurdi' etc. Perhaps the most outstanding feature of Arabic cooking is its rich almost limitless 'mezzeh table'. It is here that the Arab has lavished his culinary genius. Plate after plate of small hors d'oeuvres appear together with dips, purées, pickles (torshi), falafel (small vegetable rissoles); ful (Egyptian brown beans); fried livers, chopped, with garlic and tomatoes or simply grilled with cumin; hummus-bi-tahina (the classic chickpeas dip); aubergines – pickled or fried; courgettes, olives and peppers grilled over charcoal etc. Many items are not of Arab origin, such as stuffed vine leaves, kibbeh-neyeh (raw meat with cracked wheat) – no true Muslim should eat raw meat – or lahma-bi-ageen, or even kibbeh dishes in general, which are probably Assyrian-Armenian by origin, pre-dating Islam by centuries.

A mezzeh table is the pride of Arabic cuisine, closely followed by the sweets. Arabs have a penchant for things sweet and of all the Middle Eastern peoples they have the most exquisite and rich repertoire of desserts and drinks; and since by religious law an Arab is not permitted to indulge in intoxicating drinks, he has over the ages created an unending list of 'sherbets' made of lime, almonds, dates, oranges, liquorice etc.

As a rule olive-oil-based dishes come from Syria and Lebanon, while in Iraq alya (sheep's or lamb's tail fat) is used. The Arabians normally boil their meat in water with a little butter or fat, while samna (clarified butter made from buffalo's milk) is also very popular in Iraq.

The Arabs use a large variety of spices – understandably

so, since the Middle East was the spice route for millennia, bringing the exotic spices of India to Greece, Rome, and later to Christendom. The attarine (spice shop), usually on a small street in a corner of the local *souk*, contained all the spices imaginable. Yet once again local tastes vary. In Syria the most popular spices are cumin, coriander, cinnamon, dill, sumak, nutmeg and allspice. In Egypt the favourite is taklia (ground coriander fried with crushed garlic or a combination of coriander and cumin). In Iraq the national spice is probably turmeric, closely followed by saffron – both reflecting an Indo-Iranian origin.

In Arabia in general very little spice is used except on the eastern coastline and in the Yemen where fenugreek, hot chillies, curry powder and cinnamon are highly prized.

A feature of great interest in Arabic cuisine is the extensive and clever use of nuts. Nuts of course – once again – pre-date the introduction of Islam, since the ancients – the Greeks, Romans, Persians, Medes and Armenians – were highly versed in their usage. Their descendants have merely continued that tradition. The Syrians and Lebanese like to stuff their vegetables, poultry or lamb with pine-kernels or to thicken their sauces with almonds. The Egyptians would rather use walnuts, while the Iraqis prefer hazelnuts.

Yogourt is widely used throughout the Arab world especially in Syria and Lebanon. Yogourt, of course, is of non-Arab origin, its home ground being Iran, Caucasus and Turkey.

I have omitted many recipes for the basic reason that they are not Arab but are of foreign extraction. In this category fall a great number of oil-based vegetable dishes, together with others such as kuftas (minced meat cooked with vegetables in the oven). Also not included are the many kinds of dumplings which are of Turkish origin, eg boereg-type dishes, and several dishes making use of fruit, which though popular in the medieval recipes of Al-Baghdadi are in fact of Aryan origin (ie Iranian-Caucasian). I have also omitted several stuffed vegetable dishes as well as mussaka and pasta-type dishes, or burghul (cracked wheat) dishes since these also are essentially of non-Arab extraction.

What is left, however, I hope will give a good idea of the range, choice and variety of Arabic cuisine – a cuisine that is based on tradition and love of nature. 'Eat and drink, and let the world go to ruin,' and when you 'feed the mouth, the eyes will be bashful',[32] for the Koran has written 'Eat and drink with pleasure for what you did. Reclining on thrones set in linen and we shall join them to pure beautiful ones . . .'

After a cup of good strong Arab coffee, perhaps a sweet baklava or kulwashkur or a few minutes inhaling a narguilehs (hubble-bubble) and a few pleasantries with one's host – 'Shukran Allah' ('thanks to God') for providing our daily bread, thanks to nature, to our host and may fortune smile on him, may his children grow as wise as he and may his fathers' souls rest in peace – it is time to depart, for 'our coffee is finished, our story is finished'.

Notes

1. The Hebrew's word 'Arabbia' means dark land or steppeland, and 'Erebh' means mixed, unorganized, ie nomadic and are the nearest one can get to unravelling the true name. Incidentally, the name 'Hebrew' is probably derived from 'Abhar' – to move or to pass.
2. 'Semitic' – from them the son of Noah, the reputed ancestor of most of the people of Arabia, as well as Hebrews, Assyrians, Armenians; also applies to those who speak or spoke a form of ancient semitic language of which Hebrew and Arabic are the two modern representatives.
3. 'Race' – as defined by the Oxford English Dictionary is: 'A group of persons connected by common descent', or: 'regarded as of common stock'. It is not a cultural group.
4. J. B. Glubb, *A Short History of the Arab People*, London 1969, Hodder and Stoughton.
5. ibid.
6. J. L. Burkhardt, *Arabic Proverbs*, London 1830, Curzon Press.
7. Ebla. C. Bermand and M. Wertzman. The discovery of a vast archive casts new light on the history of the region and the advanced civilization

in Syria which predated Biblical history. This archive appears to have
been a major source for Biblical history.

8. J. B. Glubb, *A Short History of the Arab People*, London 1969, Hodder and Stoughton.
9. ibid.
10. The Koran.
11. The Koran.
12. Archbishop Cyrus was an orthodox Christian and was hated by the people who chiefly belonged to the Monophysite sect. The Christians were to pay tribute to the conquerors but were to be free to practise their own religion.
13. P. Hitti, *Makers of Arab History*, London 1937, Macmillan.
14. From 861–974 thirteen puppet Khalifs were appointed, of whom five were murdered, three were blinded and five died a natural death.
15. T. E. Lawrence, *Seven Pillars of Wisdom*, London 1935, Jonathan Cape.
16. Ockley, *History of the Saracens*, Bohn's Editions.
17. ibid.
18. Khaldoon, Abdul Rahman ibn, *Mugaddima, Kitab-el-Ibar* (in Arabic). Lebanon 1935.
19. A. J. Arberry, *A Baghdad Cookery Book*, from *Islamic Culture* No. 13, 1939. Maxime Rodinson *Recherche sur les documents Arab relatifs à la cuisine*, from *R.E. Islamiques*, 1949–50 Nos. 17–18.
20. E. Ashtor, *A Social and Economic History of the Near East in the Middle Ages*, London 1976, Collins.
21. ibid.
22. Marlowe, *Tamburlaine the Great*, part III.
23. J. L. Burkhardt, *Travels in Arabia*, London 1829.
24. *Hymn to Rain* by Badr Shakiv-al-Seyyed, 1926–1964.
25. *Histoire des Armeniens d'Alep*, Volume II, Arch. A. Surmeyan, 1946 Beirut.
26. J. L. Burkhardt, *Arabic Proverbs*. Kombar and Kyky are names of birds.
27. An Arab saying.
28. A Palestinian folk song. Anon.
29. Arab expressions.
30. The exact day and month of any festival varies because the Muslim calendar (Hegira) is based on a lunar month cycle which also means that the exact day of a given festival will differ from country to country.
31. Arab saying.
32. Arab sayings.

The Mezzeh Table

HUMMUS-BI-TAHINA	*Ground chickpeas with tahina*
MUTABBAL	*Puréed aubergine with tahina*
ABOU GANOUJE	*Grilled aubergines with tomatoes, onions and spices*
TABOULEH	*Burghul and vegetable salad*
FATTOUSH	*Bread salad*
TA'AMIA or FALAFEL	*Spicy chickpea rissoles*
EL FUL (FUL MEDAMES)	*Egyptian brown beans*
BEID HAMINE	*Hard-boiled eggs*
LABNA	*Cream cheese dip*
MAAYI	*Turnips cooked with beetroot*
MUHAMARAH	*Pomegranate and walnut dip*
ZAHTAR	*Nuts and spices dip*
KIBBEH NIYA	*Raw meat with burghul*
EGGEH	*Arab-style omelette*
EGGEH BEYTHAT	*Fried hard-boiled eggs*
BEID MAHSHI	*Stuffed eggs*
TAHINIYEH	*Garlic and tahina dip*
LSANAT MATABBLI	*Tongue salad*
TORSHI KHIAR	*Pickled cucumbers*
TORSHI BETINGAN	*Pickled aubergines*
SALATAH ARABIYEH	*Arab salad*
SALATAH-BI-TAHEENEH	*Salad with tahina*
SALATAH-BI-LABAN	*Salad with yogourt*

KIBBEH TARABLOUSIEH	*Meat and burghul stuffed with minced meat*
HAMUD SHAMI	*Chicken and garlic dip*
MI'LAAQ YEGLLI	*Fried liver with cumin*
SAMBOUSEK	*Cheese or meat pasties*
SFEEHA	*Meat tarts*
SALATAH	*Avocado salad*
SALATAH MOUKH	*Brain salad*
HAB-EL-JOSE	*Walnut balls*
MICHOTETA	*Cheese and cucumber salad*
BETINGAN MAKBOUSS	*Aubergines in olive oil*

HUMMUS-BI-TAHINA
Ground chickpeas with tahina

This traditional dip – a must on any mezzeh table – is one of the most popular and best known of all Syrian dishes, one that has in recent years been equally popularized in Europe and America. The reasons? Very simple; it has a marvellous aroma, blends extremely well with most meat dishes, especially kebabs, and the taste of tahina, garlic, lemon and cumin with mashed-up chickpeas makes this purée – in my opinion – one of the truly original classics of the Arabian cuisine. It is normally eaten with pita bread, or Shapati, or Khubz-saj (very thin Lebanese bread).

450 g (1 lb) chickpeas, soaked in cold water overnight
1 teaspoon bicarbonate of soda
3 cloves garlic, peeled
300 ml (½ pint) tahina paste
1 teaspoon chilli powder
3 teaspoons salt
2 teaspoons cumin
Juice of 2–3 lemons
Garnish
A little red pepper, cumin, lemon juice, olive oil and chopped parsley

1 Place the drained chickpeas and bicarbonate of soda in a large saucepan and three-quarters fill with water.
2 Bring to the boil, then lower the heat and simmer until the chickpeas are tender, removing surface scum from time to time. Add more boiling water if necessary.

3 Drain the chickpeas into a sieve and wash very thoroughly under cold water.

4 Set aside a few whole chickpeas for use as garnish.

5 The chickpeas now have to be reduced to a thick paste or purée. The easiest way to do this is to use a liquidizer. If you do not have one then use the time-honoured mortar and pestle. You will find it necessary to add a little water to make liquidization easier but take care not to overdo it or the purée will become too thin.

6 While liquidizing the chickpeas add the cloves of garlic – this will ensure that they are properly ground.

7 Empty the purée into a large bowl, add all the remaining ingredients and mix thoroughly.

8 Taste and adjust seasoning to your liking.

To serve

Use either individual bowls or a large serving dish. Whichever you choose, smooth the hummus with the back of a soup spoon from the centre out to the edge of the bowl so that there is a slight hollow in the middle.

Decorate in a star pattern with alternating dribbles of red pepper and the brownish-yellow cumin. Pour a little olive oil and lemon juice into the centre and then garnish with a little chopped parsley and the whole chickpeas.

8–10 servings

MUTABBAL
Puréed aubergine with tahina

This Syrian-Lebanese speciality is another must for the mezzeh table. It is a dip, similar in principle to Hummus-bi-tahina, but using grilled aubergines instead of chickpeas. It is easy to make and is traditionally eaten with bread – pita, khubz-saj or any other. Personally, I prefer to dip my kebab meat into it and I can assure you that the result is simply delicious!

2 large aubergines
3 cloves garlic, crushed
1 teaspoon salt
60–90 ml (2–3 fl oz) tahina paste
Juice of 2 lemons
1 teaspoon chilli powder
1 teaspoon cumin
1 tablespoon olive oil
Garnish
A few black olives
2 tablespoons chopped parsley

1 Make two or three slits in each aubergine with a sharp knife and cook them over charcoal, or in a hot oven, until the skins are black and the flesh feels soft when poked with a finger.
2 Allow aubergines to cool and then peel off the skin, rescuing any flesh that gets stripped off with the skin.
3 Put the flesh into a large bowl and mash with a fork.
4 Add the crushed garlic and salt and continue to mash or pound the mixture until it is reduced to a pulp.
5 Add the tahina, lemon juice and chilli powder and mix thoroughly.
6 Spoon the mixture on to a large plate, smooth it over and sprinkle with the cumin.
7 Pour the olive oil over the top and garnish with the chopped parsley and black olives.

4–6 servings

ABOU GANOUJE
Grilled aubergines with tomatoes, onions and spices

This is a regional dish from northern Syria, especially Aleppo, and was most probably introduced there by the Armenians of Cilicia as it is very much like a dish of theirs called Sumpoogi Aghtsan. It is a cold, spicy salad of cooked aubergine flesh with chopped salad vegetables and flavoured with garlic, lemon and cumin. Simple to prepare, it will keep in the refrigerator for a few days. It makes an excellent accompaniment to all grilled or roast meats and is also eaten on its own with any kind of Arab bread.

    4 medium-sized aubergines
    1 green pepper, cut into thin strips
    4 tomatoes, very thinly sliced
    1 small onion, thinly sliced
    2 cloves crushed garlic
    1 teaspoon salt
    ½ teaspoon chilli powder
    2 heaped teaspoons cumin
    4–6 tablespoons olive oil
    Juice of 2 lemons
    2 tablespoons chopped parsley

1 Pierce each aubergine once or twice with a sharp knife and place whole and unpeeled in a hot oven until they feel soft when poked with a finger and the skins are black.
2 Remove from the oven and leave until cool enough to handle.
3 Peel off the skin, put the flesh into a bowl and chop.
4 Add the sliced green pepper, tomatoes and onion.
5 Mix separately the spices with the olive oil and lemon juice, then pour over the vegetables and mix together thoroughly.
6 Stir in the parsley, taste and adjust the seasoning if necessary.
7 When serving, garnish with a little more chopped parsley.

6 servings

TABOULEH
Burghul and vegetable salad

A refreshing salad of finely chopped vegetables mixed with
burghul and having the sharp flavour of mint and lemon. A
must on any mezzeh table, this is traditionally eaten either
with lettuce leaves or bread. I prefer the former. This recipe
is popular throughout Syria, Lebanon and parts of Jordan.
A pleasant dish of great antiquity, I would like to think it
perhaps has Phoenician origins.

> 75 g (3 oz) fine burghul
> 1 cucumber, peeled and finely chopped
> 4 tomatoes, finely chopped
> 1 green pepper, seeded and finely chopped
> ½ onion, finely chopped
> 4 tablespoons chopped parsley
> 2 tablespoons dried mint or finely chopped fresh mint
> 1 teaspoon salt
> Juice of 2–3 lemons
> 4 tablespoons olive oil
> 1 lettuce, preferably cos, washed

1 Rinse the burghul in a large bowl several times until the
  water you pour off is clean.
2 Squeeze out any excess water.
3 Put the chopped vegetables, parsley and mint into a large
  mixing bowl and add the burghul.
4 Stir in the salt, lemon juice and olive oil.
5 Mix well together, leave for 15 minutes and then taste and
  adjust seasoning if necessary.
6 Arrange the lettuce leaves around the edge of a serving
  plate and pile the salad into the centre.
7 The ideal way to eat this is to make a parcel of tabouleh
  by folding a little of it in a lettuce leaf or a piece of pita
  bread.

6–8 servings

FATTOUSH
Bread salad

This is a much loved Syrian peasant salad with an unusual
texture. It was one of my childhood favourites and I have
never forgotten the thrill of eating Fattoush whenever we
visited the Arab villages where my father had friends. I have
eaten a lot of Fattoush since those days but somehow the
taste of it when prepared by the Sheik's daughters in those
happy innocent days in the richly abundant orchards under
the walnut trees on a late summer's day will – unfortunately
– never be repeated. Now for practicalities. Fattoush can be
prepared in advance and then chilled, but do not stir in the
toasted bread until just before serving or it will lose its crisp-
ness which is the whole essence of the dish.

1 large cucumber, chopped
1 lettuce heart, shredded
5 tomatoes, chopped
10 spring onions, chopped
1 small green pepper, chopped
1 tablespoon chopped fresh coriander leaves
1 tablespoon finely chopped parsley
½ tablespoon finely chopped fresh mint
1 clove garlic, crushed
6 tablespoons olive oil
Juice of 2 lemons
½ teaspoon salt
¼ teaspoon black pepper
5 thin slices of bread, lightly toasted and cut into small
cubes

1 Place all the ingredients, except the bread, in a large
  mixing bowl.
2 Toss the salad so that all the vegetables are coated with
  the oil and lemon juice.

3 Chill until ready to serve and then stir in the bread cubes and serve immediately.

6 servings

TA'AMIA or FALAFEL
Spicy chickpea rissoles

'Beans have satisfied even the great Pharaohs' – Egyptian saying.

This is one of Egypt's national dishes, popular throughout the Mediterranean coastline of the Middle East. I have emphasized the coastline because it was not known in such places as Iraq, Arabia or the Gulf States until recently when it was introduced by Palestinian and Syrian migrant workers. It is a lenten dish of the Christian Copts (who are probably the direct descendants of the Ancient Egyptians) who during religious festivals, and especially Lent when they are not allowed to eat meat for 40 days, prepare Ta'amia daily and distribute it to friends, neighbours and relatives. Today throughout Egypt, Israel, Lebanon and Syria there are small falafel shops on a 'fast chain' principle serving falafel for breakfast, lunch or supper. Ta'amia was traditionally made with Egyptian broad beans (ful nabed) but today chickpeas are usually used. There are falafel 'ready mixes' available but I think they are, to put it mildly, just not good enough. Falafel are a must on any mezzeh table and this recipe makes about 20.

450 g (1 lb) chickpeas, soaked overnight and then cooked until tender
90 ml (3 fl oz) water
1 egg, lightly beaten
1 teaspoon salt
½ teaspoon black pepper
½ teaspoon turmeric

2 tablespoons chopped fresh coriander leaves or parsley
½ teaspoon cumin
½ teaspoon cayenne pepper
1 clove garlic, crushed
1 tablespoon tahina paste or olive oil
50 g (2 oz) fresh white breadcrumbs
50 g (2 oz) flour
Sufficient oil for deep frying

1 Mince the chickpeas twice and place in a large mixing bowl.
2 Add the water, egg, salt, black pepper, turmeric, coriander leaves, cumin, cayenne pepper, garlic, tahina paste or oil and the breadcrumbs.
3 With your hands combine all the ingredients into a soft, but firm, mixture.
4 Form the mixture into 2·5 cm (1 in) diameter balls and roll them in the flour.
5 Heat the oil in a large pan and when it is hot add a few of the rissoles and fry for 3–4 minutes or until golden brown.
6 Remove the rissoles from the oil and place on kitchen paper to drain.
7 Repeat until all the rissoles are cooked.
8 Serve hot.

8–10 servings

EL FUL (FUL MEDAMES)
Egyptian brown beans

> 'It has two parts and a strong skin,
> Allah be praised!
> How do we Arabs call it?
> El Ful.'

Riddle

A traditional Egyptian dish, claimed by the Copts and probably as old as the Pharaohs. It is a simple, peasant dish that is now beloved by everyone. It is sold in small 'ful shops' in the bazaars as well as in 5-star luxury hotels and expensive restaurants. I well remember eating ful on the way to school in Aleppo – a few spoonfuls of ful and a piece of bread for a few pence. We had to queue and wait our turn then a few quick mouthfuls – how I loved that sauce – and off to make room for the next person to devour what I now regard as one of the 'greats' of Middle Eastern cuisine. The broad beans can be bought from most continental or Middle Eastern stores. There are also tinned versions of Ful Medames on the market and of these I prefer the Egyptian brands. Accompany this dish with bread and a tahina salad.

   675 g (1½ lb) Egyptian brown beans, soaked overnight
      and then drained
   3 cloves garlic, crushed
   2 tablespoons olive oil
   Juice of 2 lemons
   1 teaspoon salt
   ½ teaspoon black pepper
   4 hard-boiled eggs, shelled
   2 tablespoons finely chopped parsley

1 Preheat the oven to 130°C (250°F, Gas Mark ½).
2 Place the beans in a flameproof casserole and cover them with water.
3 Bring to the boil then place in the oven and bake for 4–7 hours, depending on the quality of the beans. At the end of the cooking time the beans should be soft but not broken up.
4 Drain the cooking liquid from the beans and discard it.
5 Stir in the garlic, olive oil, lemon juice, salt and pepper.
6 Spoon the bean mixture into 4 soup bowls and place a hard-boiled egg on top of each one.

7 Sprinkle the parsley thickly over the top and serve immediately.

10–15 servings on the Mezzeh Table
4 servings if eaten as a savoury

BEID HAMINE
Hard-boiled eggs

These are boiled eggs with a difference. The difference lies in the delicate flavour which the slow process of cooking and the inclusion of onion skins. Onion skins have traditionally been used, by Christians, to colour eggs for the Easter festivities. I am sure however that the colouring process is much older and perhaps dates as far back as the Sumerians, Hurrians and Pharaohs. I remember my grandmother filling up a large pan with onion skins and slowly cooking the eggs so that, on Easter Day, we could play the game of 'Champion Egg'. This is where two people each hold an egg in the palm of one hand. One person knocks one end of his egg against the end of the other person's egg. The winner is the one whose egg remains undamaged and he receives the loser's egg. I always lost, until the time I found out that my cousins and friends cheated. They very cleverly emptied the egg by syphoning out the contents through a small hole in the shell and then replacing it with liquidized plaster of Paris or some similar material. So when the egg was coloured it looked perfectly normal, but soon became a 'champion egg'. One of my cousins once won over 250 eggs in this way. Who says cheating doesn't pay? The eggs can nowadays be multi-coloured by the use of dyes.

Water
12–15 eggs
Skin of several onions (if ground coffee is added the colour of the eggs will be darker)

2–3 tablespoons oil
Cumin
Salt

1 Half fill a large pan with cold water.
2 Carefully add the eggs.
3 Add the onion skins – and ground coffee if you want a darker colour.
4 Sprinkle the oil over the water – this helps cut down the rate of evaporation.
5 Cook very slowly on the lowest possible heat for 5–6 hours.
6 Serve the eggs as appetizers on a mezzeh table or to top a dish of El Ful (see page 50).

I prefer my Hamine eggs dipped in salt and cumin powder and accompanied by various pickled vegetables.

12–15 eggs

LABNA
Cream cheese dip

I am often asked 'What does an Arab eat for breakfast?' The first thought that comes to my mind is Labna which is spread on a plate, with a little oil over the surface and a sprinkling of mint and paprika across the top. Labna should be garnished with a few black olives and eaten with hot bread, eg pita or khubz-saj. Labna is a must on any mezzeh table. It is refreshing, healthful and can be kept in the fridge for several days. Basically Labna is dried yogourt.

1 Prepare the yogourt (see page 236).
2 Pour or spoon the yogourt into
  (a) a colander lined with damp muslin or fine cotton cloth; or
  (b) a drawstring bag about 30 × 30 cm (12 × 12 in) made from a piece of muslin or fine cotton cloth.

3 Leave the colander in the sink or hang the bag above the sink and allow the whey to drain away.
4 What remains in the bag 5–6 hours later is a light, soft, creamy yogourt which is more like a cheese.

Lebanese and Jordanians often shape this cheese into little balls the size of a walnut, sprinkle them with a little olive oil and paprika and then make a hearty breakfast out of them.

10–15 servings approximately for the mezzeh table

MAAYI
Turnips cooked with beetroot

When I wrote to my aunt, who lives in Baghdad, to say that I was writing a book on Arab cooking she replied instructing me to be sure not to forget Maayi. Maayi, she informed me, is the 'fish and chips' or 'falafel' or even 'Kentucky chicken' of Iraq. It is sold from barrows in the main streets of Iraqi towns. 'Maayi, maayi, helweh maayi!' the young vendors cry; one can purchase a plate of hot turnips at any time of the day and then munch one's way to or from work with pleasure.

It is a simple dish to prepare and makes a colourful addition to the mezzeh table. I was instructed not to discard the cooking juices since, according to my aunt, they are very good to drink as an aid to digestion.

    12–15 turnips, or as many as are required
    6–8 small cooked beetroot
    Salt
    Water

1 Wash and peel the turnips and cut into 1 cm ($\frac{1}{2}$ in) pieces
2 Cut the beetroot into quarters.
3 Half fill a large saucepan with boiling water and season with salt.

4 Add the turnips and beetroot and simmer for 30–45 minutes or until the turnips are tender.
5 Drain the vegetables and discard the beetroot.
6 Arrange the turnips on a plate, sprinkle with a little salt and serve hot. Turnips cooked in this way should have a sweet beetroot flavour and a delicate pinky-red colour.

12–15 servings

MUHAMARAH
Pomegranate and walnut dip

This recipe from Northern Syria – the region of Aleppo – is piquant, hot and makes unusual use of the local ingredients, eg pomegranate juice, walnuts and cumin. It is excellent as an appetizer but also good as an accompaniment for all kinds of cooked meat, especially roast or kebab lamb. As it is strong and extremely hot, dip your pieces of meat, bread or biscuit into it cautiously! A must on any mezzeh table. This dip is probably of Cilician-Armenian origin where it is known as 'Garmeroug'.

  2 tablespoons red chilli pepper
  150 ml (¼ pint) olive oil
  25 g (1 oz) stale dry breadcrumbs
  1 tablespoon pomegranate juice (if available) or 1 tablespoon lemon juice
  175 g (6 oz) ground walnuts
  1 teaspoon ground cumin
  1 teaspoon allspice
  Salt to taste

1 Place the chilli pepper in a bowl and moisten with 2 tablespoons of water.
2 Add all the remaining ingredients and mix thoroughly until well blended.

3 Spoon the mixture into a small bowl and garnish with a little chopped parsley.
4 Place in the refrigerator to chill for a few hours.

About 4 servings but it is very, very hot so the number of servings depends on taste. It will keep for some time.

ZAHTAR
Nuts and spices dip

This is a popular speciality throughout the Middle East. In Egypt it is called Dukkah, while it is better known as Zahtar in Syria, Lebanon, Jordan and Iraq. It is normally served at breakfast time or on the buffet table as an appetizer. Nowadays it can be bought ready packed and usually consists of a mixture of the following ingredients – wild marjoram, sesame seeds, coriander seeds, cinnamon and chickpeas. In essence it is a dip. The ingredients can vary for as well as those mentioned above hazelnuts, walnuts etc can be used.

225 g (½ lb) sesame seeds
100 g (¼ lb) coriander seeds
100 g (¼ lb) walnuts
100 g (¼ lb) chickpeas – the most suitable are those which you can buy in many delicatessens and which are pre-cooked, salted and dried
3 tablespoons ground cumin
1 teaspoon salt
½ teaspoon black pepper
1 tablespoon cinnamon
2 tablespoons crushed dried wild marjoram
1 tablespoon sumak powder

1 Roast or grill separately the sesame seeds, coriander seeds, walnuts and chickpeas.
2 Pound them together until they are finely crushed, but do

not pulverize them or the oils from the nuts and seeds will be released and will start to form a paste. The essence of this dip is that it is a mixture of DRY ingredients.

3 Mix all the ingredients together in a large bowl, taste and adjust the seasonings to your own liking.

4 Arrange a little of the zahtar on one plate and pour a little olive oil on to another plate.

5 To eat, dip a piece of bread first into the oil and then into the zahtar. Try it for breakfast with a cup of tea or coffee – it is extremely refreshing.

10–20 servings, but when mixed it can be stored in an air-tight container for months.

KIBBEH NIYA
Raw meat with burghul

There are two outstanding versions of this dish: (a) Houm Miss, or Kibbeh Niya Armeni, where the meat-to-burghul proportions are more or less even and the kibbeh is divided into smaller portions and eaten after dipping into a special hot cooked meat and nut mixture; (b) Kibbeh Niya where there is twice as much raw meat to burghul.

The Lebanese have made Kibbeh Niya one of their national dishes. However, this is certainly a non-Muslim dish and I believe it to be pre-Christian and probably of Assyrian origin. Interestingly enough Steak Tartare is not too dissimilar to Kibbeh Niya – at least in principle.

Muslims are not permitted by their religious laws to eat raw meat and I must confess I am more partial to the Houm Miss version than the recipe below, since I find that the meat–burghul ratio is more balanced and palatable, and that the addition of cooked meat and nuts, ie the hot–cold relationship, more exciting. But let me not denigrate Kibbeh Niya, beloved of millions of Lebanese and Syrians who swear by it and rate a woman's femininity by her ability to prepare a kibbeh dish. A glass of arak and some cos lettuce leaves are superb accompaniments.

You can purchase burghul (cracked wheat) from most continental shops. Buy the fine version for this dish, which is best made just before you are ready to eat it.

50 g (2 oz) fine burghul
Salt to taste
Black pepper to taste
100 g (4 oz) very lean lamb, minced twice
1 tablespoon very finely chopped onion
1 tablespoon olive oil
Pinch of chilli powder
1 teaspoon pine kernels
Garnish
A bowlful of cos lettuce leaves
1 onion, quartered

1 Wash the burghul in a large bowl until the water you pour off is clean.
2 Tip the burghul on to a large plate or baking sheet, season with the salt and black pepper and knead for 5 minutes, wetting your hands if the mixture sticks to them.
3 Add the minced lamb and chopped onion and knead for a further 5–10 minutes until the mixture is smooth. Keep wetting your hands if it makes the kneading easier.
4 Spread the kibbeh mixture over a large plate and press until smooth, forming a slight depression in the centre.
5 Pour the olive oil into the surface of the kibbeh and sprinkle a little chilli powder all over the surface.
6 Sprinkle the pine kernels over the top.
7 Serve immediately accompanied by the lettuce leaves and onion.

4–6 servings

EGGEH
Arab-style omelette

One of the interesting features of the Arabic cuisine is the Eggeh. Eggeh is an egg dish with a meat, vegetable or pasta filling. It can be served hot or cold as a first course or, in large helpings, as a main dish. It is an extremely popular dish for picnics and pilgrimages and religious festivals.

Eggeh is not an omelette in the accepted sense of the word since the eggs in it are acting as a binding for the various fillings and not, as with omelettes proper, the main ingredient with the fillings as extras to give added flavour or colour. This particular recipe comes from Syria and uses olive oil for the cooking. However butter or samna (clarified butter) are commonly used to cook eggeh in regions where olive oil is not easily available – eg in Iraq, the Gulf States and Egypt.

There are special frying pans or 'eggeh pans' available, made of copper, but a 'rock cake' tin will do perfectly well.

3 teacups chopped parsley
$1\frac{1}{2}$ teacups chopped onion
3 level tablespoons crushed dried mint
6 large eggs, beaten
1 tablespoon self-raising flour
2 cloves garlic, crushed
2 teaspoons salt
$1\frac{1}{2}$ teaspoons black pepper
Olive oil or cooking oil

1 Mix together all the ingredients, except the oil, in a large bowl until well blended. The mixture should be thick and you can add more chopped parsley and onion if necessary.
2 One-third fill each section of the cooking tin with the oil and place over a low heat.
3 When the oil is hot put 1 tablespoon of the eggeh mixture

into each section and cook gently until each eggeh is set and the undersides are a golden brown.

4 Turn each with a fork and continue cooking until the other side is also golden.

5 Remove each eggeh as and when cooked. If necessary add a little more oil to each section of the cooking tin and continue the process until all the mixture is cooked.

The mixture can also be cooked as one large omelette in a frying pan. Although they can be eaten hot I prefer eggeh cold. Incidentally, they make excellent fillings for sandwiches.

Makes 35–40. Serves about 8 as an hors d'oeuvre.

EGGEH BEYTHAT
Fried hard-boiled eggs

In this recipe the eggs are hard-boiled first, then fried and finally rolled in a mixture of spices and served as an hors d'oeuvre or with vegetables or meat. There is a recipe by al-Baghdadi who advises to hard-boil the eggs, fry in oil and then roll in a mixture of coriander, cinnamon and cumin.

This is a very popular dish throughout the Arab world, particularly in Egypt and, naturally, Baghdad where one can see these eggs on sale at street corners.

    4 hard-boiled eggs (or as many as are required)
    Olive oil or cooking oil
    2 teaspoons cinnamon
    2 teaspoons turmeric
    2 teaspoons cumin
    1 teaspoon coriander
    Salt and pepper to taste

1 Shell the hard-boiled eggs.

2 With a pin, prick the eggs through the white all over (to just reach the yolk). This will prevent the eggs splitting and also help the flavours to penetrate.
3 Place the spices in a large bowl and mix thoroughly.
4 Heat the olive oil (or cooking oil) in a deep pan.
5 Drop each egg carefully into the oil, lower the heat and fry until the eggs are browned all over – do not overcook.
6 Remove the eggs by means of a large spoon and roll them in the spice mixture.
7 You can serve the eggs hot or as an accompaniment to meat or vegetable dishes. I have found that Eggeh Beythat makes an excellent appetizer and is a must on any mezzeh table.

4 Eggs

BEID MAHSHI
Stuffed eggs

'Trifles become treasures to the poor' – Arab saying.

This is a delightful recipe, given to me by a Palestinian artist friend whose mother was an excellent cook. The salad dressing is a Western touch. I prefer to use a yogourt and cinnamon sauce (see page 216).

4 hard-boiled eggs
1 tablespoon finely chopped parsley
1 small onion, finely chopped
3 tablespoons olive oil
Salt and pepper to taste
$\frac{1}{2}$ teaspoon cinnamon
Lettuce leaves
Pinch red pepper
Salad dressing of your choice or yogourt and cinnamon sauce (see page 216)

Garnish
A little finely chopped parsley

1 Shell the eggs and cut them in half lengthways.
2 Remove the yolks and place in a bowl.
3 Mash the yolks with a fork and then mix in the parsley and onion.
4 Add the olive oil, a little at a time, and continue mixing.
5 Season to taste with the salt, pepper and cinnamon.
6 Take up a little of the mixture in a spoon and roll it between your palms to form a small ball. Place it in one half of an egg white.
7 Repeat the process until all the yolk mixture is used up and all the egg whites are filled.
8 Arrange the filled egg halves on a bed of lettuce leaves and sprinkle with the red pepper.
9 Spoon the salad dressing or yogourt–cinnamon sauce over the top and then sprinkle with the parsley.

8 egg halves

TAHINIYEH
Garlic and tahina dip

Tahina is a cream made from sesame seeds. It is a great favourite in the Arab world, particularly in Syria, Lebanon and Jordan. Tahina was known to the Hittites and Urartians and was extensively used by the ancient Cappadocians and Cilicians as was noted by the Greek historian Xenophon in *The Persian Expedition* (430–354 BC).

150 ml (¼ pint) tahina paste
Juice of 2 lemons
300 ml (½ pint) milk
2 cloves garlic, crushed
1 tablespoon finely chopped parsley

1 teaspoon salt
½ teaspoon chilli powder
50 g (2 oz) white breadcrumbs
Garnish
1 tablespoon finely chopped parsley
½ teaspoon cumin
Sliced hard-boiled eggs (Beid Hamine, see page 52)

1 Pour the tahina into a bowl and stir in the lemon juice. The mixture will become very thick.
2 Slowly add the milk, stirring until you have obtained a thick creamy consistency.
3 Add the garlic, parsley, salt and chilli powder. Taste and adjust seasoning if necessary.
4 Add the breadcrumbs and mix thoroughly.
5 Pour the mixture into a serving bowl and sprinkle with the parsley and cumin.
6 Serve as a dip accompanied by hard-boiled eggs.

Tahiniyeh will keep in a covered container for several days in the refrigerator. It can be used as a salad dressing. Stir 3–4 tablespoons of the mixture into 225 g (½ lb) cooked, diced beetroot or 225 g (½ lb) cooked, sliced carrots and then garnish with a little chopped parsley.

6 servings

LSANAT MATABBLI
Tongue salad

This is a Lebanese-Syrian salad very popular both in the villages and the seaside restaurants. It is always accompanied by a glass of arak and pita bread. Traditionally an olive oil and lemon juice dressing is poured over the tongues, but in Lebanon a tahina dressing (similar to the Tahiniyeh dip, but substituting water for milk) is often used instead.

6 small lambs' tongues
1 onion, peeled and quartered
1 clove garlic
1 stick celery, washed and cut into 1 cm (½ in) slices
1 clove
2 bay leaves
1 teaspoon salt
3–4 peppercorns, crushed
2 tablespoons olive oil ⎫   or 3–4 tablespoons of
1 tablespoon lemon juice ⎭   tahina dressing (see
                            Tahiniyeh, page 62)

Garnish
2 tablespoons finely chopped parsley
½ teaspoon paprika
wedges of lemon

1 Wash the tongues under cold running water then place
  them in a large saucepan and add sufficient water to cover.
2 Add the onion, garlic, celery, clove, bay leaves, salt and
  crushed peppercorns.
3 Bring to the boil, cover and simmer for about 1 hour or
  until the tongues are tender.
4 Leave to cool and then peel each tongue by carefully
  cutting one edge and removing the skin with your fingers.
5 With a sharp knife cut each tongue into slices about 3 mm
  (⅛ in) thick.
6 Arrange the slices decoratively on a plate and chill for at
  least 1 hour.
7 Mix together the oil and lemon juice in a small bowl and
  pour this mixture over the tongue (or pour over the tahina
  dressing).
8 Garnish with the parsley, paprika and lemon wedges.

6 servings

TORSHI KHIAR
Pickled cucumbers

'It is written upon the cucumber leaf, "he who watches during the night sleeps during the day, he who passes the night in fun is unfit for business during the day".'

Arabic Proverbs, J. L. Burkhardt

Pickling is a big business in the Arab world where, even today, grocers prepare their own pickles. There are some who specialize solely in pickling all types of vegetables, eg turnips, onions, cauliflowers, cabbage, sweet or hot peppers, cucumbers, aubergines etc. There is a small dark shop in the old *souk* of Damascus where I was flabbergasted to find almost every conceivable vegetable and fruit pickled, as well as small birds such as snipe, sparrow and thrush.

The Middle Eastern method of pickling is simple. The raw vegetables are washed, scrubbed or peeled and packed tightly into a jar. The vinegar and spices are then added and the jar is covered and tightly sealed. Pickles are prepared in large quantities and are a must on any mezzeh table or as an accompaniment to main dishes.

The two recipes I have included are for small cucumbers and small aubergines. In the Middle East these vegetables are pickled whole. The proportion of vinegar to water varies from grocer to grocer and family to family. A good combination is 3 parts brine to 1 part vinegar. I have found that large glass jars like those you can sometimes still find in sweet shops are ideal. Otherwise a plastic container will do.

900 g (2 lb) small pickling cucumbers (ask your green-
   grocer to order some specially for you)
4 cloves garlic
1 teaspoon dill seed
4–6 black peppercorns
4–6 whole coriander seeds

75–100 g (3–4 oz) salt
300 ml (½ pint) vinegar, malt or white wine
900–1200 ml (1½–2 pints) water (depending on size of
    container)

1 Scrub the cucumbers thoroughly and pack them in a large
  glass jar or plastic container.
2 In a large bowl mix together all the remaining ingredients
  and then pour the mixture over the vegetables.
3 If the vegetables are not completely covered top up with
  water.
4 Seal the jar tightly and leave in a warm place for about 2
  weeks.
5 Before serving the pickles rinse them under cold running
  water.

Eaten as required, the cucumbers will keep for months.

TORSHI BETINGAN
Pickled aubergines

'A vinegar seller does not like another vinegar seller' (imply-
ing that picklers do not like comparisons made about their
products) – Arabic saying.

This is my favourite torshi. My grandmother used to make
jars of these pickles when in season and we feasted throughout the year on pickled aubergines on their own as a mezzeh
or accompanying kebabs and other main dishes. The
aubergines should be small and thin.

900 g (2 lb) small, thin aubergines
4 cloves garlic, finely chopped
2 small, dried chilli pepper pods, finely chopped
2–3 celery leaves with stalks, finely chopped
100 g (¼ lb) green, shelled walnuts, ground
600 ml (1 pint) water

3 tablespoons salt
450 ml (¾ pint) vinegar, malt or white wine

1 Wash the aubergines, remove the stalks, but do not peel them.
2 Make an incision about 2·5 cm (1 in) long down each aubergine.
3 Drop the aubergines into a large saucepan of boiling water. Simmer for 10 minutes and then drain.
4 In a small bowl mix together the garlic, chilli, celery and walnuts.
5 Push a little of this mixture into the incision in each aubergine.
6 Arrange the aubergines in a large glass jar or plastic container.
7 Mix the water, salt and vinegar together and pour this mixture over the aubergines.
8 Fasten the jar or container to make it airtight and leave for 3–4 weeks in a warm place.
9 Before serving rinse the aubergines under cold, running water.

Eaten as required, the aubergines will keep for months.

SALATAH ARABIYEH
Arab salad

'Did but the radish digest its own self!' (Radishes facilitate the digestion of other food, but they themselves remain indigestible in the stomach.) – Egyptian saying.

In the small dark eating houses of old Jerusalem most meat dishes are accompanied by a salad popularly known as Salatah Arabiyeh. Below are three versions of this salad – plain; with tahina; with yogourt. The ingredients can vary according to taste and availability, but prepare this dish as near as possible to the time of serving.

Salad

1 green pepper, thinly sliced
1 onion, finely sliced
3 tomatoes, cut into thin wedges
4 radishes, thinly sliced
1 clove garlic, finely chopped
2 tablespoons finely chopped parsley
4–5 coriander seeds, crushed; or ½ teaspoon ground
    coriander
Salt and pepper to taste
1 teaspoon dried mint
Arabiyeh dressing
3 tablespoons olive oil
Juice of 1 lemon

1 In a large salad bowl mix together the green pepper,
  onion, tomatoes, radishes, garlic and parsley.
2 Mix the remaining ingredients together and pour over the
  salad.
3 Toss gently and serve immediately.

4–6 servings

SALATAH-BI-TAHEENEH
Salad with tahina

1 Use the same salad ingredients as above.
2 Make a Taheeneh dressing by mixing the juice of 1 lemon
  with 4 tablespoons of tahina paste and 150 ml (¼ pint)
  water until smooth.
3 Pour this dressing over the vegetables, toss gently and
  serve immediately.

4–6 servings

SALATAH-BI-LABAN
Salad with yogourt

1 In a large salad bowl mix together the green pepper, onion, tomatoes, radishes, garlic and parsley.
2 Mix the remaining Arab salad ingredients together with 300 ml (½ pint) yogourt.
3 Pour this dressing over the vegetables, toss gently and serve immediately.

4–6 servings

KIBBEH TARABLOUSIEH
Meat and burghul stuffed with minced meat

Filling
25 g (1 oz) pine kernels or 25 g (1 oz) chopped walnuts
225 g (8 oz) minced lamb
1 onion, chopped
1 teaspoon each salt, black pepper and allspice
1 tablespoon chopped parsley
Kibbeh
225 g (½ lb) fine burghul
450 g (1 lb) very lean lamb, minced twice
2 tablespoons very finely chopped onion
2 teaspoons salt
1 teaspoon black pepper

Oil for deep frying
Lemon wedges for garnish

1 To make the filling first fry the nuts in a little oil. Remove from the pan and drain.
2 Add the meat to the pan and cook for about 15 minutes, stirring frequently.
3 Add the onion and seasonings and cook for a further 15–20 minutes.

4 Stir in the nuts and parsley and set the mixture aside.

5 To prepare the kibbeh, first wash the burghul in a bowl and pour away the excess water.

6 Spread the burghul on a baking tray and knead for a few minutes.

7 Add the lean minced lamb, finely chopped onion and seasonings and knead together for at least 10–15 minutes, keeping your hands damp with cold water.

8 To make the stuffed kibbeh, first wet your hands and break off a piece of kibbeh about the size of an egg.

9 Hold the ball of kibbeh in the palm of one hand and with the index finger of the other hand make a hole in the kibbeh.

10 Press the index finger down into the palm of the other hand squeezing out the kibbeh and making the shell a little thinner.

11 Slowly rotate the ball of kibbeh so that the finger is continually pressing down on a new part of the kibbeh shell and making it thinner.

12 Continue turning the shell round and round and pressing it up the finger until you have a long oval shape with a slightly wider mouth. The art is to get the shell as thin as possible without cracking it. It will be easier to do so if you keep your hands damp.

13 Place a tablespoon of the filling into the shell and then close the opening by drawing the edges together and sealing.

14 Wet your hands again and roll the kibbeh between your palms to smooth it off and ensure that it is a real oval shape.

15 Continue this process until you have used all the kibbeh mixture and the meat filling.

16 To cook, add sufficient oil for deep-frying to a large pan and set to heat.

17 Add a few kibbeh at a time and fry until golden brown all over.
18 Remove and drain.
19 Serve hot accompanied by lemon wedges.
20 To eat, cut the kibbeh in half and squeeze lemon juice over the meat filling.

About 6–8 servings depending on their size. They will keep 2–3 days in the fridge, or will freeze well.

HAMUD SHAMI
Chicken and garlic dip

An unusual appetizer of Damascus origin, but more popular with northern Egyptians. It is also served as an accompaniment to cold meats or chicken, but more often than not I have seen it eaten as an appetizer dip with bread or lettuce leaves. It has a very beautiful translucent appearance with a light golden yellow colouring.

1 tablespoon vegetable oil
3 cloves garlic, finely crushed
1 pint chicken stock
5 tablespoons ground rice
150 ml (¼ pint) water
Juice of 1 lemon
¼ teaspoon turmeric
¼ teaspoon ground saffron

1 Heat the oil in a saucepan, then add the garlic and fry until golden yellow.
2 Add half the chicken stock to the pan and mix well.
3 In a bowl mix together the ground rice and the water.
4 Pour this mixture into the saucepan and add the remaining stock, stirring constantly.
5 Reduce the heat to very low and cook, stirring constantly, until the sauce becomes very thick.

6 Add the lemon juice, turmeric and saffron, stir well and bring the mixture to the boil.

7 Either serve hot as an accompaniment to a cold meat dish or pour into a bowl and chill in the refrigerator to serve as a mezzeh.

6 servings

MI'LAAQ YEGLLI
Fried liver with cumin

A fabulous and highly popular dish from Northern Syria which often appears on the mezzeh tables of sophisticated restaurants. It is simple to prepare, cheap and highly nutritious. It can be eaten hot, but is more successful when allowed to cool first.

450 g (1 lb) lamb's liver (calf's liver will also do)
3 tablespoons olive oil
Juice of 1 lemon
½ teaspoon salt
½ teaspoon black pepper
2 bay leaves
Oil for frying
Garnish
2 tablespoons finely chopped parsley
1 small onion, thinly sliced into rings
1 tablespoon cumin powder
Lemon wedges

1 Wash the liver under cold running water then dry with kitchen paper.

2 Cut into slices 1 cm (½ in) thick, removing all the sinews.

3 Mix together in a large bowl the oil, lemon juice, salt, pepper and bay leaves.

4 Add the liver pieces and leave to marinate for at least 1 hour.

5 Drain the liver on kitchen paper.
6 Heat some oil in a large pan and fry the liver slices for 4–5 minutes. Do not overcook.
7 Arrange the slices on a plate, garnish with the parsley and onion rings and sprinkle with the cumin. Serve with lemon wedges.

6 servings

SAMBOUSEK
Cheese or meat pasties

If thou would'st know what food gives most delight,
Best let me tell, none hath subtler sight.
Take first the finest meat, red, soft to touch,
And mince it with the fat, not overmuch;
Then add an onion, cut in circles clean,
A cabbage, very fresh, exceedingly green.
And season well with cinnamon and rue,
Of coriander add a handful too.
And after that of cloves the very least,
Of finest ginger, and of pepper best.
A handful of cumin, murri just to taste
Two handfuls of Palmyra salt . . .
Then, as thou wilt, in pastry wrap it round,
And fasten well the edges firm and sound . . .
Pour in the frying pan the choicest oil
And in that liquor let it finely broil . . .

> *In Praise of Sambousek* by the court musician-poet Isbag ibn Ibrahim of Mosul who practised at the time of the great Haroun-al-Rasheed. This translation is by A. J. Arberry from Ali ibu Hasan Al Masoodi's *Maroojial Dhahab (les Prairies d'or)*

These delicious pasties are known throughout the Arab world and beyond. Highly popular in Syria, Lebanon and Iraq, they are called Samsak in my father's city of Kilis in southern Turkey while in distant north India the dish Samosa is undoubtedly based on the principle of frying meat or vegetables in dough. The Turkish Beureg are again a variation on the Sambousek theme. Here then is a typical recipe from Jordan making use of either a cheese or a meat filling.

Dough
225 g (½ lb) plain flour
60 ml (2 fl oz) oil
2 tablespoons melted butter
60 ml (2 fl oz) milk
1 teaspoon sugar
Cheese filling
225 g (½ lb) feta cheese (available in most continental stores)
2 tablespoons finely chopped parsley
½ tablespoon dillweed
Meat filling
Oil for frying
1 small onion, finely chopped
225 g (½ lb) minced meat
1 teaspoon salt
½ teaspoon allspice
½ teaspoon cinnamon

1 egg, beaten
Sesame seeds

1 If using the cheese filling then crumble the cheese with a fork in a small bowl and stir in the parsley and dill, until it has the consistency of a paste.
2 If using the meat filling then heat the oil in a saucepan, add the onion and sauté until soft. Add the meat and cook for 5 minutes, stirring occasionally. Season with

the salt, allspice and cinnamon, stir well, cover and cook over a low heat for 15–20 minutes. Remove from the heat and leave to cool.

3 To make the dough, sift the flour into a mixing bowl and make a well in the centre.

4 Into this pour the oil, butter and milk, add the sugar and stir with your hand until the mixture forms a soft, greasy ball.

5 Sprinkle some flour over a worktop and roll out the dough until it is about 3 mm (⅛ in) thick.

6 Cut into rounds about 7·5 cm (3 in) in diameter.

7 Now put a teaspoon of the filling of your choice in the centre of one half of each circle.

8 Dip your finger in cold water and run it around the edge of the pastry and then fold over the other half of each circle to form a half-moon shape.

9 Seal the edges either by pinching with your fingers or pressing with a fork.

10 Arrange the pasties on a lightly greased baking sheet.

11 Brush each with the beaten egg and sprinkle liberally with the sesame seeds.

12 Place in an oven preheated to 180°C (350°F, Gas Mark 4) and cook for about 40 minutes until golden brown and well risen.

13 Serve either hot or cold.

12–15 pasties (allow 2–3 per person)

SFEEHA
Meat tarts

'His bread is kneaded and his water is in the jug' – Arab saying.

Any self-respecting mezzeh table should have a few sfeehas adorning it. They are small, round 10 cm (4 in) circles of dough topped with a mixture of meat, nuts and vegetables. They can be served open or closed and are often accompanied by natural yogourt. They are popular throughout Syria and Iraq; the famed Lahmajoon of the Armenians is related to Sfeeha, but is not the same.

This is an Iraqi recipe that does not include tomatoes or tomato purée, but has pomegranate juice instead. This can be purchased from some Middle Eastern shops, but if not available then substitute sumak powder. This gives the tarts a lemony tang.

Dough
600 ml (1 pint) lukewarm water
1 tablespoon dried yeast
900 g (2 lb) plain flour
1½ tablespoons salt
3 tablespoons olive oil
Filling
3 tablespoons olive oil or butter
75 g (3 oz) pine kernels
1 onion, finely chopped
900 g (2 lb) lean minced meat
1 small green pepper, finely chopped
4 tablespoons finely chopped parsley
1 tablespoon pomegranate syrup or 1 tablespoon sumak powder
½ teaspoon allspice
½ teaspoon cayenne pepper
1 teaspoon salt
¼ teaspoon black pepper
Garnish
Lemon wedges

1 First prepare the dough. Measure 4 tablespoons of the water into a small bowl, sprinkle the yeast over the top and let it rest for 3 minutes.
2 Stir to dissolve the yeast completely and set to one side.
3 Sift the flour and salt into a large mixing bowl, make a well in the centre and pour in the yeast mixture.

 4 Add the olive oil and 450 ml (¾ pint) of the remaining water.
 5 Slowly stir in the flour until well mixed and the dough can be gathered into a ball. If the dough is a little thick then add a little more water.
 6 Sprinkle a table or worktop with some flour.
 7 Place the dough on the table top and commence kneading with your hands. Do this by pressing the dough down, pushing it under with the heels of your hands and folding it back on itself until the dough is smooth and elastic. Sprinkle it with a little flour now and again to prevent it sticking to the table.
 8 Shape the dough into a ball, place in a clean bowl, cover with a cloth and leave in a warm place for about 1 hour.
 9 The dough should have about doubled in size. Punch it down with your fist and divide it into about 15 pieces.
10 Roll each piece into a ball about 3·5 cm (1½ in) in diameter.
11 Set aside for about 30 minutes.
12 Meanwhile prepare the filling. Heat 1 tablespoon of the oil in a saucepan and fry the pine kernels for 1–2 minutes.
13 Add the onion, meat, green pepper, parsley, pomegranate syrup (or sumak powder), allspice, cayenne pepper, salt and black pepper.
14 Mix thoroughly, taste and adjust seasoning if necessary.
15 Set aside.
16 Now roll each dough ball into a circle about 10 cm (4 in) in diameter and 3 mm (⅛ in) thick.
17 Spoon about 6 tablespoons of the filling on to the centre of each round.
18 With your fingers spread the filling to within 1 cm (½ in) of the edge of each round and bring the edge up slightly.
19 Brush some baking sheets with olive oil.
20 Arrange the tarts on the sheets and bake in a preheated oven 180°C (350°F, Gas Mark 4) for 20–30 minutes or until the pastry is lightly browned. Do not overcook.
21 Serve hot accompanied by yogourt.

To make closed Sfeeha
Spoon about 6 tablespoons of the filling on to the centre of
each round then pull up the edge from 3 equally distant
points to make a triangular-shaped pie. Using your fingers
or the teeth of a fork, pinch the dough securely together at
the top. Cook as for open sfeeha.

Approximately 15 tarts

SALATAH
Avocado salad

This is reputed to be one of the oldest dishes in the world.
The Egyptian Copts claim it as theirs and, since they are probably the true descendants of the Pharaohs, their claim is
most probably right. Tomatoes, of course, must have been a
later addition since they did not appear in the old world until
the sixteenth and seventeenth centuries. Do use cos lettuce if
available as most European varieties are not known in the
Middle East.

> 2 ripe or over-ripe avocados
> 2 tomatoes, finely chopped
> 1 small onion, finely chopped
> 1 teaspoon salt
> 1 teaspoon paprika
> ½ teaspoon black pepper
> Juice of 1 lemon
> 1 cos lettuce, thoroughly washed
> 1 tablespoon fresh chopped parsley

1 Wash the avocados.
2 Peel and cut into small pieces.
3 In a deep saucepan mash the avocados, tomatoes and
  onion with the back of a large spoon or a pestle.
4 Add the paprika, salt and pepper, pour on the lemon juice
  and stir well.
5 Line the bottom and sides of a salad bowl or a large plate
  with the cos lettuce leaves.

6 Add the avocado salad to the centre of the salad bowl and garnish with the chopped parsley.
7 Cool in a refrigerator for 30 or more minutes and serve.

4 servings

SALATAH MOUKH
Brain salad

'What do you expect from such a man, you can't even fry his brains' – Arab saying.

A wonderful appetizer which is popular throughout the Middle East amongst all the various nationalities. There are certain variations, but basically the recipes are the same. The Middle Eastern people are the masters of lamb and goat cookery. Through the ages they have evolved a cuisine that makes use of every bit of the animal so that nothing is discarded. Brains are considered a great delicacy and are sold in small kiosks in every major city as well as in small cafés as an accompaniment to a glass of arak. You should be able to order them from your butcher.

4 lambs' brains
Salt
Vinegar
4 spring onions, thinly sliced including heads
Juice of 1 lemon
Black pepper
$\frac{1}{2}$ teaspoon cumin
Garnish
Cos lettuce leaves
Pinch paprika
1 tablespoon finely chopped parsley
Few lemon wedges

1 Soak the brains for about 1 hour in cold water containing the salt and vinegar.
2 Place the sliced onions in a small bowl, add the lemon juice and leave to marinate.

3 Remove the thin skin (outer membranes) of the brains very carefully.
4 Wash under cold running water.
5 Place the brains in a saucepan and cover with water seasoned with 1 teaspoon salt and 1 tablespoon vinegar.
6 Bring to the boil and simmer for about 15 minutes.
7 Drain and dry the brains.
8 Slice the brains with a sharp knife.
9 Arrange the lettuce leaves over a large plate and place the brain slices over them.
10 Stir the olive oil into the onion–lemon juice mixture and then add the salt and black pepper to taste and the cumin.
11 Sprinkle this mixture over the brains.
12 Garnish with the paprika and parsley and add lemon wedges if you like a really lemony flavour.

4–6 servings

HAB-EL-JOSE
Walnut balls

These delightful walnut balls will embellish any mezzeh table. They are one of the specialities of the city of Antakya (the famed Antioch of Greek, Roman and Crusader fame in northern Syria), now part of Turkey. A very simple and quick dish to prepare.

150 g (5 oz) walnuts, ground
50 g (2 oz) breadcrumbs
$\frac{1}{2}$ teaspoon cumin
Tahina
$\frac{1}{2}$ teaspoon cayenne pepper
Salt to taste
Olive oil to grease fingers
50 g (2 oz) sesame seeds
Garnish
Pinch of paprika

1 In a bowl mix together the walnuts, breadcrumbs and cumin.

2 Add sufficient tahina to make a soft paste.
3 Add the cayenne pepper and salt to taste.
4 Now grease your fingers with the oil and break the paste
   into small pieces.
5 Shape into round walnut-sized balls.
6 Pour the sesame seeds on to a plate and roll each walnut
   ball in them.
7 Arrange the balls decoratively on a round plate and place
   a toothpick in each.
8 Sprinkle with paprika.

Makes about 20

MICHOTETA
Cheese and cucumber salad

A traditional salad from Egypt especially popular among the
Greeks and Copts of Cairo and Alexandria. It is an excellent
appetizer. The cheese is usually feta which is easily found in
most continental or Indian shops. As a substitute cottage
cheese or curd cheese will do as well. The Egyptians usually
eat this salad with their great favourite – Ful Medames (see
page 50). Eat by dipping a piece of bread into it, accompanied by a glass of arak.

225 g (½ lb) cheese, eg feta or cottage cheese
Juice of 1 lemon
2 tablespoons olive oil
½ large cucumber, peeled and diced
1 onion, finely chopped
½ teaspoon cumin
Salt and black pepper
Garnish
Pinch of paprika

1 Place the cheese in a salad bowl with a tablespoon or two
   of water and crumble with a fork.
2 Slowly add the lemon juice and olive oil.
3 Add the cucumber, onion, cumin and mix well.

4 Season to taste with salt and pepper.
5 Garnish with the paprika.

4–6 servings

BETINGAN MAKBOUSS
Aubergines in olive oil

A Syrian speciality, the aubergines are pickled in olive oil
and eaten as a mezzeh. They are simple to prepare and very
tasty. Cut them lengthways when serving. Other vegetables –
eg cucumbers, small marrows, lemons and limes – can be
pickled in the same way.

    12 or more small aubergines
    2 teaspoons salt
    5–6 tablespoons walnuts, coarsely chopped
    2 teaspoons paprika
    4 lemons, thinly sliced
    Olive oil or corn oil

1 Drop the aubergines into a large pan of boiling water and
   cook for about 10 minutes.
2 Drain and dry them with kitchen paper.
3 With a knife make an insertion lengthways from the stalk
   end about one third of the full length of each aubergine.
4 Mix together the salt, walnuts and paprika.
5 Spoon a little of the walnut mixture into each insertion,
   followed by a lemon slice.
6 Arrange the aubergines carefully in layers in a glass jar
   and fill with olive oil.
7 Close the jar tightly and leave for 3 weeks. By this time the
   aubergines will be soft and fragrant.

Use as required

Soups

MELOKHIA	*Traditional Egyptian soup*
CHOURBA-BI-KOUSA	*Courgette and milk soup*
LABANEYAH	*Spinach and yogourt soup*
CHERVAH	*Lamb soup with rice*
CHOURBA-FUL-SUDANI	*Peanut soup*
SHREET ADS MAJROOSH	*Lentil soup with cumin*
CHOURBA-AL-KIBBEH	*Soup with kibbeh balls*
MUNAZELET BANADOORA	*Onion and tomato soup*
MAKHLOUTA	*Rice and lentil soup*

MELOKHIA
Traditional Egyptian soup

'He put him into the basket of Melokhia, he came out of the basket of Badenjan' – Arab proverb.

Melokhia is a classic of the Egyptian cuisine. I emphasize Egyptian since it is much older than that of the Arabs, Greeks or Romans. There are frescoes portraying the cooking of melokhia on Pharaonic tombs.

Throughout the centuries the peasants – fellahine – have cultivated this vegetable (*corchorus olitorius*) and have virtually lived on it. Its leaves can be eaten fresh, or dried for the winter months. Although one does find melokhia in Libya, Lebanon and southern Syria it is really in the vast over-populated villages of the Nile Delta that it makes its importance felt. Here the Egyptian peasant usually eats it twice daily. There are therefore many variations of this soup and to have to choose one recipe in preference to others has been very difficult. The one I eventually selected is given here as I found it to be the most satisfactory of those I tried. It is extremely difficult to find fresh melokhia in Britain and the USA, but fortunately it is sold in its dried form in some Greek and Middle Eastern stores. The results are equally good with the dried form. However, if you cannot find melokhia, under no circumstances use spinach as recommended by some cookery writers. In my opinion if one is trying to achieve that particular flavour which is melokhia then one has no alternative but to use melokhia. There is, after all, a limit to substitution!

Stock

A chicken or a rabbit or a knuckle of beef or veal

1 onion, quartered

2 tomatoes, skinned and quartered

1 clove garlic

Salt and pepper to taste

Soup

75 g (3 oz) dried melokhia leaves or 450 g (1 lb) fresh
  leaves

3 cloves garlic

2 tablespoons butter or oil

1 teaspoon cayenne pepper

1 tablespoon ground coriander

1 First make the stock by placing all the ingredients in a
   large saucepan, covering with water and simmering for
   2–3 hours.

2 Add more water from time to time as necessary – you will
   need 1–1·75 litres (2–3 pints) of stock for the soup.

3 Remove any scum which may form and taste and adjust
   the seasoning at the end of the cooking time.

4 Strain the stock into a large saucepan.

5 Crush the dried melokhia leaves. If they are not brittle
   enough then dry them out by placing them in a warm
   oven for a few minutes.

6 Place the crushed leaves in a bowl and moisten with a
   little hot water. Set aside until they double in bulk.

7 Add them to the stock and simmer for 20–30 minutes.

8 Make the garlic sauce – Taklia – by crushing the garlic
   with a little salt and frying in the butter or oil.

9 When it turns brown add the cayenne pepper and
   coriander and stir for 2–3 minutes, forming a smooth
   paste.

10 Add this to the soup, cover and simmer for a further 2
   minutes. It is important to stir occasionally and not to

overcook as the leaves will otherwise sink to the bottom.
11 Finally, check the seasoning and adjust accordingly.

6 servings

CHOURBA-BI-KOUSA
Courgette and milk soup

'Take off the hands from the broth lest they should be burnt'
– an Egyptian saying meaning: Do not be too interested in
yourself.

This delicious courgette soup is from Lebanon and has a hint
of French cuisine about it with its use of milk and its
simplicity.

350 g (¾ lb) courgettes
600 ml (1 pint) milk
25 g (1 oz) butter
2 tablespoons flour
Salt and black pepper
2 tablespoons finely chopped parsley
Sumak powder (optional)
Turmeric (optional)

1 Wash and peel the courgettes and cut into 2·5 cm (1 in)
   chunks.
2 Half fill a large saucepan with lightly salted water and
   bring to the boil. Add the courgettes and cook until soft.
3 Drain thoroughly.
4 Mash or liquidize the courgettes to a purée and put to one
   side.
5 Bring the milk to the boil in another pan.
6 Melt the butter in a small pan, add the flour and stir until
   you have a smooth paste.
7 Now slowly add the milk to the paste, stirring all the time
   until the mixture thickens.

8 Add the courgette purée to the mixture and continue cooking and stirring until the mixture is hot.
9 Season with the salt and pepper.
10 Serve in individual bowls sprinkled with the sumak or turmeric (optional) and with the parsley.

4 servings

LABANEYAH
Spinach and yogourt soup

This is a yogourt soup – not very popular among the Arabs, at least not as much as it is with the Iranians and Armenians. It is a traditional Egyptian soup normally made with a local plant of the spinach family called 'silq' in Arabic. Spinach is equally good.

In Alexandria turmeric is added to the spinach and rice while they are cooking, whilst in Damascus sumak powder is added which gives a dark red colour as well as a piquant lemony flavour.

450 g (1 lb) fresh spinach or 225 g (½ lb) frozen spinach
2 tablespoons cooking oil
1 onion, coarsely chopped
3 spring onions, finely chopped
100 g (¼ lb) rice, washed thoroughly
About 1 litre (2 pints) water
1 teaspoon salt
Black pepper to taste
450 ml (¾ pint) yogourt stabilized with 1 egg
1 clove garlic, crushed

1 Wash fresh spinach thoroughly in several bowlfuls of cold water. If using frozen spinach then leave it to thaw out.
2 Drain the spinach and cut into large pieces.

3 Heat the oil in a large saucepan and sauté the onion until soft and turning golden.
4 Add the spring onions and spinach, stir well and sauté for a few more minutes.
5 Add the rice and water and stir.
6 Season with salt and pepper to taste, bring quickly to the boil then lower the heat and simmer until the rice and spinach are cooked – about 15–20 minutes.
7 Meanwhile, in a small bowl beat together the stabilized yogourt and the garlic and set aside.
8 When the soup is ready add the yogourt mixture and stir thoroughly.
9 Heat through, but *do not boil*.
10 Serve immediately, accompanied by bread and fresh herbs.

4 servings

CHERVAH
Lamb soup with rice

This is a traditional dish from the Arabian desert and is one of the oldest known soups of the Middle East – containing all the basic ingredients, eg lamb, rice and onion, that were available to the desert nomads. The wandering Bedouin did not have much else. The Syrian-Lebanese Chourba Mosaat is a slightly more refined and richer version of this recipe since it includes cinnamon, celery, noodles etc. It is a simple, tasty and filling soup.

25 g (1 oz) ghee or butter
1 large onion, thinly sliced
1 litre (2 pints) water
225 g (½ lb) breast of lamb, cut into 1–2·5 cm (½–1 in) cubes
2 large tomatoes, coarsely chopped

2 carrots, peeled, quartered lengthways and cut into 1 cm
　(½ in) sticks
Salt and pepper to taste
1 teaspoon dried mint
50 g (2 oz) rice, washed
2 tablespoons chopped parsley

1　Melt the ghee or butter in a large saucepan and fry the
　onion until golden brown.
2　Add the water, meat, tomatoes, carrots, salt, pepper and
　mint.
3　Simmer, covered, over a low heat until the meat is tender,
　about 45 minutes.
4　Now add the rice and cook until it is tender, about 15
　minutes.
5　Remove from the heat, pour into a tureen, sprinkle with
　the parsley and serve immediately.

4 servings

CHOURBA-FUL-SUDANI
Peanut soup

As the name suggests this is a soup of Sudanese origin. One
of the most remarkable images of my childhood which still
haunts my memory is the magnificent sight of a tall Negro in
white robes standing proud and statuesque on the corner of
the main square in Aleppo selling roasted peanuts. He was
the first black man I had ever seen. I remember the first time
we – a few kids from school – approached him with some
trepidation as he was most certainly very different from anyone we had ever seen. He spoke a kind of Arabic, had a
gentle smile and magnificent white teeth. We soon became
friends and almost every afternoon after school I spent my
few pence purchasing roasted peanuts in small cone-shaped

brown papers and exchanged a few words with 'El Soudani' as he was known. I shall never forget that sad, forlorn look of his as he stood there in the midst of that bustling, oriental city watching the carts and cars moving slowly through the narrow streets.

This soup is from southern Egypt where it borders the Sudan and it is an extremely popular dish amongst the poor villagers of the region. Normally, melted butter is used instead of cream but I prefer the latter.

450 g (1 lb) fresh shelled peanuts
600 ml (1 pint) milk
600 ml (1 pint) stock
Salt and pepper to taste
4 tablespoons double cream

1 Spread the nuts over a baking sheet and roast in a moderate oven for about 15 minutes or until the skins can be easily removed. (The time will depend on the freshness and the type of peanuts.)
2 Leave to cool.
3 Rub off the skins by gently squeezing the nuts.
4 Now pulverize the nuts, either in a blender or a mortar and pestle.
5 Place the ground nuts in a large saucepan and add the milk, a little at a time, stirring constantly.
6 Add the stock and salt and pepper to taste and bring to the boil over a moderate heat.
7 Stirring frequently, cook for about 10 minutes.
8 Remove from the heat and serve in individual bowls with a tablespoon of cream swirled into the top of each portion.

4 servings

SHREET ADS MAJROOSH
Lentil soup with cumin

Throughout the Arab world and the Middle East in general, lentil-based soups are the most popular. There are many types: plain, thick, with spinach or several vegetables, with rice or vermicelli, and even with meatballs. This Syrian recipe is a simple, tasty one flavoured with cumin and with a strong aroma of garlic.

Arabs have a custom of breaking bread into small pieces and adding them to their soup. A more attractive way of serving the soup is to make croutons by cutting a thick slice of bread into 1 cm ($\frac{1}{2}$ in) pieces and frying them in oil. Add them to the soup just before serving.

    450 g (1 lb) ads majroosh (dried, split red lentils)
    1·75 litres (3 pints) stock or water
    1 onion, quartered
    1 tomato, quartered
    1 stick celery with leaves, chopped
    1 clove garlic, coarsely chopped
    50 g (2 oz) butter
    1 tablespoon chopped onion
    2 teaspoons ground cumin
    1 teaspoon salt
    $\frac{1}{4}$ teaspoon black pepper
    Garnish
    2 lemons, cut into wedges
    Croutons

1 Wash the lentils under cold running water and drain.
2 Bring the stock or water to the boil in a large saucepan.
3 Add the lentils, onion, tomato, celery and garlic and stir.
4 Reduce the heat and simmer for 30–45 minutes or until the lentils are tender. This will depend on the age and quality of the lentils.

5 Meanwhile in a small pan melt half the butter and fry the chopped onion until golden, stirring frequently.

6 Remove the pan from the heat.

7 Purée the soup through a sieve by rubbing the ingredients through with the back of a wooden spoon and then discarding any remaining bits of vegetables. Otherwise put it into an electric blender.

8 Return the soup to the saucepan and cook for a further 5 minutes, stirring all the time.

9 Add the cumin, salt and pepper.

10 Just before serving stir in the remaining half of the butter (if you like a light soup add a little more water) and simmer for a few more minutes.

11 Serve immediately in individual soup bowls. Top with a few freshly fried croutons and sprinkle with the fried onions.

12 Serve the lemon wedges separately.

6 servings

CHOURBA-AL-KIBBEH
Soup with kibbeh balls

Kibbeh dishes are the pride of Syria and Lebanon. They are most probably of Assyrian origin. The famed Koubebis of Mosul, Tabriz, Aleppo, Karput and Baghdad show a lineage much older than the Muslim era. As burghul (cracked wheat) was known and used by the ancient Urartians of Armenia and the Assyrians of modern Syria and Iraq before the Arabs or Turks were on the pages of history, their Assyrian origins cannot really be disputed. The Persians, to date, do not use nor are they familiar with burghul. Interestingly enough the Kurds of Iraq call it Tzawour. It is Tzavar in Armenian, from Tzoren = wheat and Havar el = to beat or split into small pieces. The Arabs were, and for the most part still are, rice eaters.

There are several soups made with kibbeh such as Kibbeh-bi-Laban (kibbeh and yogourt), Kibbeh-bi-Banadoora (kibbeh and tomatoes) as well as kibbeh with chickpeas and marrows and kibbeh in pomegranate juice. The recipe below is a traditionally popular one from the Christian mountains of Lebanon.

Kibbeh
175 g (6 oz) fine burghul
350 g (12 oz) lean lamb, minced twice
1 onion, finely chopped
1 teaspoon salt
½ teaspoon black pepper
Soup
50 g (2 oz) butter
1 large onion, finely chopped
1 clove garlic, finely chopped
1·75 litres (3 pints) stock or water
2·5 cm (1 in) stick cinnamon
Salt and pepper to taste
Pinch allspice
175 g (6 oz) long-grain rice, washed thoroughly
3–4 tablespoons finely chopped parsley

1 Prepare the kibbeh mixture as for Kibbeh Tarablousieh (see page 69).
2 When the mixture is ready, dampen your palms and shape it into small marble-sized balls and then place them in the refrigerator for 30 minutes.
3 Melt the butter in a large saucepan.
4 Add the kibbeh balls, a few at a time, and fry until they are brown all over.
5 As they are cooked, set them aside to drain on kitchen paper.
6 Now sauté the onions and garlic, adding more butter if necessary.

7 Stir in the spices and the rice and fry for a few minutes stirring frequently. Now add the water or stock.

8 Bring to the boil, lower the heat and simmer for 5 minutes.

9 Add the kibbeh balls and cook for a further 15 minutes or until the rice is tender.

10 Remove the cinnamon stick and check the seasoning.

11 Just before serving stir in the chopped parsley.

8 servings

MUNAZELET BANADOORA
Onion and tomato soup

A simple straightforward soup. I have chosen this because it is typical of all Arab vegetable soups. The ingredients may vary, but the principle is the same. First the meat and vegetables are fried then they are seasoned. Stock or water is added and the ingredients are simmered until tender. Finally the soup is garnished with parsley, bread or a seasoning such as cumin, sumak, cayenne pepper etc.

This particular soup is from Syria, but is naturally well known throughout the Levant. Most Arab soups are rich in ingredients and are more like stews. People add bread slices and often make a full meal of them. Add boiled rice or Arab bread and you have a satisfying lunch or supper dish. By following this basic recipe you can substitute, and add or subtract, whatever vegetables you like or have available.

40 g (1½ oz) butter or ghee
2 onions, thinly sliced
450 g (1 lb) lamb cut into 3·5 cm (1½ in) pieces
2 cloves garlic, finely chopped
900 g (2 lb) tomatoes, chopped
1 tablespoon tomato purée
1·75 litres (3 pints) water

1 teaspoon salt
$\frac{1}{2}$ teaspoon black pepper
$\frac{1}{2}$ teaspoon dillweed
Garnish
2 tablespoons finely chopped parsley

1 Melt the butter in a large saucepan.
2 Add the onions and sauté until soft.
3 Add the meat and garlic, stir well, then cover the pan and simmer very gently for 15 minutes.
4 Add the tomatoes, stir, cover and continue cooking.
5 Meanwhile, in a small bowl dilute the tomato purée in a little of the water.
6 Add this mixture to the saucepan together with the rest of the water.
7 Add the salt, pepper and dill, stir, cover and bring to the boil.
8 Lower the heat and simmer for about $1-1\frac{1}{2}$ hours or until the meat is tender.
9 Taste and adjust the seasoning if necessary.
10 Serve immediately garnished with the parsley.

6 servings

MAKHLOUTA
Rice and lentil soup

'He's made a right Makhlouta of his life' – a Syrian saying meaning 'He has made a mess of his life.'

In Arabic 'makhlouta' means mixed or stirred, and the name of the soup comes from the fact that the rice and lentils are mixed so much during cooking that one would be unable to separate them. This is a very popular dish from Syria and is also known in southern Turkey. The Turks and Armenians use burghul instead of rice.

4 tablespoons olive oil
1 onion, finely chopped
75 g (3 oz) long-grained rice, washed
1·75 litres (3 pints) water or stock
1 teaspoon salt
½ teaspoon black pepper
1 teaspoon cumin
¼ teaspoon cinnamon
Pinch powdered cloves
175 g (6 oz) split red lentils
Pinch cayenne pepper

1 Heat the oil in a large saucepan and fry the onion until soft and just turning brown.
2 Add the rice and fry for a few minutes, stirring frequently.
3 Stir in the water or stock, the salt, pepper, cumin, cinnamon and cloves.
4 Bring to the boil and simmer for 5 minutes.
5 Now add the split lentils and stir well.
6 Lower the heat and simmer gently until the rice is tender and the lentils are cooked but not mushy.
7 Garnish with a pinch of cayenne pepper and serve immediately.

6 servings

Meat Dishes

KABAB HALABI	*Lamb kebab with yogourt*
DAOUD PASHA	*Meatballs and pine nuts in tomato sauce*
KAMOUNIAT-EL-LAHEM	*Braised steak with cumin*
MARAAK	*Meat stew*
IMMOS	*Meat and yogourt stew*
FAKHED KHAROUF YAMANI	*Yemeni leg of lamb*
KIBBEH-BI-SINIYEH	*Meat and burghul with nuts*
MANSAF	*Steak and yogourt pilav*
KAFTA MABROUMA	*Nuts with meat rolls*
SAALIK	*Lamb and rice in milk*
MANTALI	*Beef mould*
KAFTA-BIL-KARAZ	*Meatballs with cherries*
YAH HABIB FEISAL	*Liver kebab*
MILAQ MESHWI-BI-TOUM	*Grilled liver and garlic*
KHAROUF MAHSHI	*Whole roast lamb*
ROZ-BIL-HUMMUS	*Rice with meat and chickpeas*

KABAB HALABI
Lamb kebab with yogourt

This kebab comes from Aleppo in Syria, one of the great centres of Middle Eastern cooking famed for its cheese, sweets and kebabs. The cuisine of Aleppo is interesting for it has evolved through the ages absorbing Assyrian, Turkish, Armenian and Crusader influences.

900 g (2 lb) lean lamb, cut into 2·5 cm (1 in) cubes
2 tablespoons olive oil
Juice of 1 onion
3 pita bread
50 g (2 oz) butter or ghee, melted
3 large tomatoes
½ teaspoon salt
450 ml (¾ pint) yogourt
6 spring onions, finely chopped
1 tablespoon finely chopped parsley

1 Put the lamb cubes into a large bowl, add the oil and onion juice, mix well and leave to marinate for 2 hours at room temperature.
2 When you have prepared the fire and are ready to cook the kebabs, first warm the pitas for a minute or two over the fire.
3 Cut the bread into 1 cm (½ in) wide strips and place on a large platter.
4 Pour the melted butter over the bread, mix well, arrange the pieces neatly and set aside.

5 Thread the pieces of meat on to skewers and grill over charcoal for 10–15 minutes, turning frequently.

6 Meanwhile peel and chop the tomatoes.

7 Put the tomatoes into a small frying pan and cook gently for about 3 minutes.

8 Season with the salt.

9 When the kebabs are cooked first pour the tomatoes over the bread and then slide the kebabs off the skewers on to the tomatoes.

10 Pour the yogourt over the meat.

11 Sprinkle the chopped onion and parsley over the top and serve immediately.

6 servings

DAOUD PASHA
Meatballs and pine nuts coated in tomato sauce

This tasty meal is dedicated to Garabed Artin Pasha Davoudian, an Armenian by birth (1816–73) who became the first governor of Lebanon – from 1860 to 1868. He was a remarkable man who modernized the administration of the country as well as the economy. He was also the first Christian to hold such high office in the Ottoman administration.

This is a rich dish and so is best served with a plain rice pilav.

　　450 g (1 lb) minced lamb
　　1 teaspoon salt
　　¼ teaspoon black pepper
　　½ teaspoon cumin
　　1 teaspoon coriander
　　½ teaspoon allspice
　　2 tablespoons olive oil
　　1 onion, thinly sliced

2 tablespoons pine nuts or blanched almonds

2 tablespoons tomato purée blended with 300 ml (½ pint) water

½ tablespoon lemon juice

½ teaspoon dried basil

1 tablespoon butter

1 In a large bowl mix together the meat, salt, pepper, cumin, ½ teaspoon of coriander, and the allspice.

2 Shape the mixture into small balls.

3 Heat the olive oil in a saucepan, add the onion and cook until soft and lightly coloured.

4 Add the meatballs and fry for about 10 minutes, stirring occasionally until browned all over.

5 Add 1 tablespoon of nuts and fry for a further 2 minutes.

6 Pour in the diluted tomato purée and the lemon juice and add the remaining coriander and the basil.

7 Stir well to coat the meatballs with the mixture.

8 Reduce heat to low and simmer for about 30 minutes, stirring occasionally, until the meat is cooked and the sauce has thickened.

9 Turn the meatballs and sauce into a warmed serving dish and keep hot.

10 Melt the butter in a small frying pan, add the remaining nuts and cook for 2–3 minutes, stirring frequently, until they are a golden colour.

11 Stick one nut into each meatball and serve at once.

4 servings

KAMOUNIAT-EL-LAHEM
Braised steak with cumin

This is a favourite Egyptian dish. There are several variations, the simplest being one that consists of meat, garlic and cumin. Others include several types of vegetables, other spices – eg turmeric and ginger – as well as eggs in their shells. It is a dish full of flavour – especially that of cumin which I regard as one of the most characteristic spices of the Middle East. It is best accompanied by a plain rice pilav.

3 tablespoons oil
2 onions, chopped
675 g (1½ lb) stewing steak, cut into 2·5 cm (1 in) cubes
2 potatoes, diced
225 g (8 oz) chickpeas, soaked overnight and drained
2 cloves garlic, crushed
2 teaspoons ground cumin
1½ teaspoons salt
½ teaspoon black pepper
300 ml (½ pint) beef stock

1 Preheat the oven to 190°C (375°F, Gas Mark 5).
2 Heat the oil in a large frying pan, add the onions and fry until soft but not brown.
3 Add the meat to the pan and cook, stirring occasionally, until it is brown.
4 Transfer the meat and onion mixture to a flameproof casserole.
5 Add the potatoes, chickpeas, garlic, cumin, salt and pepper and stock and stir.
6 Add sufficient water to cover the ingredients and bring to the boil.
7 Cover the casserole tightly and place on the bottom shelf of the oven.
8 After 1 hour, reduce heat to 130°C (250°F, Gas Mark ½) and leave the casserole to cook for 6 hours.
9 Serve directly from the casserole.

4–6 servings

MARAAK
Meat stew

'The best food is that which fills the belly' – Arab saying.

This is a very simple peasant dish from Iraq which is popular throughout the country, especially in the south. Clever use is made of coriander and the meal is usually served with a plain boiled rice. The Arabs do not much care for sauces since many of them used to – and some still do – eat with their fingers. Maraak is a dry stew and it should be cooked slowly. In the past the peasants used lamb or mutton fat instead of butter. Clarified butter or ghee will do very well instead. Yogourt or a fresh mixed salad go extremely well with this dish.

50 g (2 oz) ghee or clarified butter
3 onions, coarsely chopped
900 g (2 lb) lamb, cut into 5 cm (2 in) pieces
450 g (1 lb) tomatoes, coarsely chopped
1 teaspoon salt
½ teaspoon black pepper
½ teaspoon paprika
1 tablespoon ground coriander
Garnish
2 tablespoons finely chopped parsley

1 Melt the ghee or butter in a large saucepan, add the onions and sauté for a few minutes until light brown.
2 Add the meat pieces and sauté, turning occasionally, until nicely browned.
3 Add the tomatoes, salt, pepper, paprika and coriander.
4 Stir well and bring to the boil.
5 Lower the heat, cover and cook for 1–1½ hours or until the meat is tender, stirring frequently.
6 Pour into a serving dish and garnish with the parsley.
6 servings

IMMOS
Meat and yogourt stew

A Lebanese speciality, immos literally means 'cooked in his mother's milk' – suggesting the tenderness of the meat in use. This is a rich and creamy dish and is usually served with a plain rice pilav and a crisp salad.

   300 ml (½ pint) water
   1 tablespoon oil
   2 onions, sliced
   900 g (2 lb) leg of lamb, cut up into 5 cm (2 in) pieces
   1 teaspoon salt
   ½ teaspoon black pepper
   2 cloves garlic, crushed
   1 teaspoon chopped fresh parsley stalks
   600 ml (1 pint) yogourt
   1 tablespoon cornflour mixed to a paste with 1 tablespoon water
   Grated rind of 1 lemon
   1 tablespoon chopped fresh coriander or parsley

1 Bring the water and oil to the boil in a large pan.
2 Add the onions, meat, half the salt, the pepper, garlic and parsley stalks.
3 Cover the pan, reduce heat and simmer gently until the lamb is tender and the liquid has been reduced by two-thirds.
4 Place the yogourt and the cornflour mixture in a saucepan with the remaining salt and bring gently to the boil, stirring constantly.
5 Reduce the heat to very low and cook for 8–10 minutes.
6 Add the yogourt mixture and the lemon rind to the lamb mixture and simmer, uncovered, for a further 15 minutes.
7 Pour the mixture into a large serving dish and sprinkle with the coriander or parsley.

6 servings

There was a man who had a very sneering, dirty and rapacious wife. Whatever food he brought home, the wife would consume it and the man kept silent. One day he brought home some meat in honour of a guest who would be arriving. His wife ate it up with kebab and wine. When the man came in he said to her 'Where is the meat?' 'The cat has eaten the meat,' she replied. 'Go and buy some more meat.' The man told his servant 'Bring the scales, I will weigh the cat.' He weighed it. The cat was half a 'mann' (local measure). Then the man said 'Oh deceitful wife. The meat was half a mann and one sitir over. The cat is just half a mann. If this is the cat then where is the meat? Or if this is the meat, where is the cat? Search for her!'

Mathnawi al Rumi, *Proverbs*

FAKHED KHAROUF YAMANI
Yemeni leg of lamb

The Yemen, tucked away in the south-west corner of Arabia between the Indian Ocean and the Red Sea, is a land of stark mountains and deserts with a few fertile valleys. One of these – and the greatest – is Wadi Hadhramant which was once an ancient South Arabian kingdom which lived off the trading of incense and spices. This civilization, which lasted over 1500 years, began to crumble away as sea traffic replaced the overland caravan routes and as the religion of the Yemenites, who worshipped the Sun, the Moon and Venus (Ashtar), was replaced by that of Mohammed.

Yemen today, apart from its political divisions, is also a poor, backward land still maintaining its ancient traditions and famed for its native coffee, dried fish and Gumumi tobacco – much prized in Arab countries for smoking in 'narguilehs' (hubble bubbles).

There is a strong Indian and south Asian influence throughout the land and this is also reflected in the cuisine.

1·5–1·75 kg (3–4 lb) leg of lamb, boned
2 tablespoons oil

$\frac{1}{2}$ teaspoon salt
$\frac{1}{4}$ teaspoon black pepper
$\frac{1}{4}$ teaspoon thyme
$\frac{1}{4}$ teaspoon rosemary
1 tablespoon chopped fresh mint or 1 teaspoon dried mint
$\frac{1}{2}$ teaspoon sugar
$\frac{1}{4}$ teaspoon ground cumin
2–3 bay leaves
4 cloves

1 Lay the lamb out flat.
2 Brush it with the oil and sprinkle with the salt and pepper.
3 Mix the thyme, rosemary, mint, sugar and cumin together and rub into both sides of the meat.
4 Place the bay leaves and cloves inside the lamb.
5 Roll up the leg and secure with string.
6 Place the leg in a roasting tin, brush with the oil and place in an oven preheated to 230°C (450°F, Gas Mark 8).
7 After 15 minutes reduce temperature to 190°C (375°F, Gas Mark 5) and cook for a further $1\frac{1}{4}$ hours or until the meat is tender. Baste it occasionally with its own juices.
8 Serve with a simple rice pilav and/or fresh salad.

6–8 servings

KIBBEH-BI-SINIYEH
Meat and burghul with nuts

'Allah in all His wisdom gave rice to the Ajems (Persians), burghul to the Ermens (Armenians), cous-cous to the Meghrebys (North Africans) and to us He only gave El-Ful' – Arab saying.

A traditional dish from the burghul (cracked wheat) lands of Turkey, Syria and Lebanon. Burghul was the predecessor of rice, which is only grown in certain parts of the Middle East, basically Iran, Iraq and South-Eastern Turkey. In the rest of the Middle East wheat dishes predominated until recent times. Very little burghul is used now in Arab cooking, except in such dishes as the Kibbehs which are still popular, more with the non-Muslim Lebanese, Assyrians and Armenians. In short, burghul is a non-Arab cereal.

This dish can be baked in advance and warmed in the oven when needed. A fresh bowl of salad and natural yogourt are good accompaniments.

Filling
25 g (1 oz) pine kernels or 25 g (1 oz) chopped walnuts
175 g (6 oz) minced lamb
½ onion, chopped
1 teaspoon each of salt, black pepper and allspice
1 tablespoon chopped parsley

Kibbeh
225 g (½ lb) lean lamb, minced twice
100 g (4 oz) fine burghul
1 tablespoon very finely chopped onion
1½ teaspoons salt
1 teaspoon black pepper
Pinch allspice
50 g (2 oz) butter
2 tablespoons oil mixed with 4 tablespoons water

1 To make the filling, first fry the nuts in a little oil and then remove from the oil and drain.
2 Add the meat to the oil and cook for about 15 minutes, stirring frequently.
3 Add the onion and seasoning and cook for a further 15–20 minutes.
4 Stir in the nuts and parsley and set the mixture aside.
5 Heat the oven to 190°C (375°F, Gas Mark 5).

6 To prepare the kibbeh, first wash the burghul in a bowl and pour away the excess water.

7 Spread the burghul out on a baking sheet and leave for 5–10 minutes.

8 Add the lean minced lamb, finely chopped onion and seasoning and knead together for at least 10–15 minutes, keeping your hands damp with cold water.

9 Divide the mixture into 2 parts.

10 Butter a shallow, circular baking dish about 20 cm (8 in) in diameter and sprinkle it with a pinch of allspice.

11 With your fingers spread one half of the burghul mixture evenly over the bottom of the dish.

12 Spread the filling evenly over this.

13 Arrange the remaining burghul mixture evenly over the top.

14 Wet your hands and press the mixture well down on to the filling.

15 Wet a sharp knife and run it around the edge of the dish to loosen the kibbeh.

16 Cut the kibbeh into diamond shapes.

17 Place a small dab of butter on each diamond.

18 Pour the oil and water over the top.

19 Bake in the oven until golden brown and crisp around the edges.

4 servings

MANSAF
Steak and yogourt pilav

900 g (2 lb) stewing steak cut into 5 cm (2 in) pieces
1 onion, quartered
1½ teaspoons salt
900 ml (1½ pints) water
450 ml (¾ pint) yogourt

1 egg
2 tablespoons vegetable oil
2 tablespoons pine kernels
2 tablespoons almonds
Rice pilav, see Roz Shami (page 182)

1 Place the meat cubes, onion and salt in a large saucepan
   with the water and bring to the boil. Remove any scum
   which may appear.
2 Simmer for about 45 minutes or until the meat is tender.
   Add a little more water if necessary.
3 Remove the meat and retain the stock.
4 Pour the yogourt into a large saucepan, break in the egg
   and whisk.
5 Heat over a low heat, stirring in one direction all the
   time.
6 Slowly bring the yogourt to the boil.
7 Now add half the meat stock – about 300–450 ml
   (½–¾ pint) – to the yogourt and continue stirring.
8 Bring to the boil and remove from the heat.
9 Add the pieces of meat to the sauce, return to the heat
   and, once again, bring just to the boil.
10 Remove from the heat and keep warm.
11 Meanwhile prepare the rice as in the recipe for Roz
   Shami.
12 In a small frying pan heat the oil and gently fry the nuts.
13 To serve spread the rice over a large platter, pile the
   pieces of meat in the centre and cover with half the
   yogourt sauce.
14 Sprinkle the nuts over the top and serve the remainder of
   the sauce separately.

6 servings

KAFTA MABROUMA
Nuts with meat rolls

This recipe is included firstly because it is a family favourite and secondly because it portrays well the diverse influences on the Arab cuisine. This is a typical Cilician recipe making use of meat, spices and nuts. It is essentially simple, but absolutely marvellous with a fresh salad. It is not surprising that this is a recipe from Aleppo, northern Syria, where the people are of Greek, Crusader and Armenian origin in general and have retained a great deal of their pre-Islamic traditions.

> 1 egg
> 450 g (1 lb) lean lamb, minced twice
> 1 onion, very finely chopped
> 1 teaspoon salt
> ½ teaspoon black pepper
> ½ teaspoon cayenne pepper
> 4 tablespoons coarsely chopped walnuts
> 2 tablespoons melted butter
> ½ teaspoon sumak powder, optional
> *Garnish*
> 1 lemon cut into wedges
> 1 tablespoon chopped parsley

1 Place the egg in a bowl, beat and add the meat and onion.
2 Sprinkle in the salt, black and cayenne pepper and knead vigorously for about 10 minutes until the mixture is soft and smooth.
3 Place the mixture on a large board or floured working surface and flatten it until it is about 1 cm (½ in) thick.
4 Divide the mixture into 4 rectangles about 20 × 6–7·5 cm (8 × 2½–3 in).
5 Arrange 1 tablespoon of the chopped nuts in a row along

one of the longer sides of each rectangle 5 mm ($\frac{1}{4}$ in)·
away from the edge.

6 Roll up each rectangle to form a long sausage.

7 Lightly butter a baking tray and arrange the rolls on it
   side by side.

8 Pour the remaining butter over the top and sprinkle with
   the sumak powder.

9 Add 2–3 tablespoons of water to the tray and place in an
   oven preheated to 190°C (375°F, Gas Mark 5).

10 Bake for about 1 hour or until the rolls are cooked
    through.

11 Serve garnished with the lemon wedges and parsley.

4 servings

SAALIK
Lamb and rice in milk

Saalik means 'poor', 'beggar' and also 'robber'. Perhaps the
only true rice dish of the Arab, it originates from the heart of
Arabia (modern Saudi Arabia). It basically consists of the sole
ingredients that are available in the desert – rice, meat and
milk. For thousands of years the Bedouins have feasted on
this dish and even today, in the vast stretches of the desert
where large numbers of these people still live almost
untouched by the passing of time, this true food of the
nomad is cherished and it is regarded as a great honour to be
treated to a supper of Saalik accompanied by honey or syrup
which is stirred into the food. I would suggest that you
accompany the dish with a fresh salad since it is a pleasing
contrast to the rich, sweet flavour of the Saalik.

1 small, 1–1·5 kg (2–3 lb) leg of lamb
1 onion, finely chopped
$\frac{1}{2}$ teaspoon salt
$\frac{1}{4}$ teaspoon black pepper

4 cloves (optional)
½ teaspoon dillweed (optional)
450 ml (¾ pint) milk
350 g (12 oz) rice, washed thoroughly and drained
100 g (4 oz) butter

1 Place the leg of lamb in a large, deep saucepan, cover with water, bring to the boil and simmer.
2 Add the onion, salt and pepper and the cloves and dill if you are using them and simmer for about 2 hours or until the meat is tender.
3 Remove the meat from the stock and keep warm.
4 Measure the stock. You need 450 ml (¾ pint) and if there is not enough then make it up with water.
5 Return the stock to the saucepan, add the milk and bring quickly to the boil.
6 Add the rice to the stock, lower the heat, cover and simmer until the rice is tender and the liquid absorbed.
7 Melt the butter in a small saucepan.
8 Serve the rice on a large platter, pour the melted butter over it and arrange the meat on the top.

6 servings

MANTALI
Beef mould

A popular dish throughout the Arab world, but especially in Jordan, southern Syria and Saudi Arabia. Although traditionally made with beef, minced lamb is often substituted nowadays.

The traditional vegetables used are carrots, French beans and Syrian truffles, but the latter is almost always substituted nowadays by mushrooms. The Egyptians also love to use bakla – broad beans. Double cream is a rather new addition since in the past either yogourt or milk was used or, in some areas, kaymak – the thick cream of the Arab.

50 g (2 oz) ghee or butter
50 g (2 oz) plain flour
300 ml (½ pint) stock
675 g (1½ lb) stewing steak, trimmed of fat and minced 2–3 times
1½ teaspoons salt
½ teaspoon black pepper
½ teaspoon allspice
½ teaspoon cayenne pepper
2 eggs, well beaten
150 ml (¼ pint) double cream
2 carrots, peeled and thinly sliced
100 g (¼ lb) French beans, cut into 2·5 cm (1 in) pieces
100 g (¼ lb) button mushrooms
Juice of 1 lemon

1 Heat the ghee or butter in a saucepan, remove from the heat and stir in the flour.
2 Reduce heat to very low, return the pan and cook for 2–3 minutes, stirring all the time.
3 Mix in the stock and continue stirring until the mixture thickens.
4 Add the meat, seasoning and spices, stir well and remove the pan from the heat.
5 Stir in the eggs, return the pan to the heat and simmer for about 5 minutes, stirring all the time.
6 Now stir in the cream and remove from the heat.
7 Pour the mixture into a well-greased ring mould, cover with foil and place in a large saucepan or casserole.
8 Add enough water to come half way up the mould, cover the pan or casserole and simmer for about 1½ hours. Top up with water if necessary.
9 Meanwhile, cook the vegetables in lightly salted, boiling

water. First the carrots and when they are nearly cooked
add the beans and when they are nearly ready add the
mushrooms and continue cooking until all the vegetables
are tender.

10 Drain the vegetables.

11 To serve, turn the Mantali out on to a large plate and fill
the centre with the vegetables.

12 Accompany with rice or boiled or roast potatoes.

6 servings

KAFTA-BIL-KARAZ
Meatballs with cherries

I first ate this dish, when still a child, in a small Syrian
village where my father had friends. The cherries came from
the village orchards and they were big, black and juicy. The
meal was served on lightly toasted bread – Khubz-saj.

The recipe below includes a tomato sauce which, although
popular in Syria, is more so amongst the Assyrians and the
Iraqis – who in part are of Assyrian origin. If you cannot
obtain fresh black cherries then use tinned ones, but double
the quantity of lemon juice to counteract the added sweetness.

900 g (2 lb) lean lamb, minced twice
450 g (1 lb) black Morello cherries, fresh or tinned, stoned
1 tablespoon salt
1 teaspoon black pepper
$\frac{1}{2}$ teaspoon cinnamon
$\frac{1}{2}$ teaspoon nutmeg
$\frac{1}{2}$ teaspoon ground cloves
6 tablespoons oil
Sauce
1 onion, finely chopped
1 clove garlic, finely chopped

4 tomatoes, coarsely chopped
450 ml (¾ pint) water
1 teaspoon salt
½ teaspoon allspice
1 tablespoon lemon juice if using fresh cherries, 2
   tablespoons if using tinned

1 Put the minced meat in a large bowl and knead until
   smooth.
2 Add the salt, pepper, cinnamon, nutmeg and cloves.
3 Knead for a few more minutes.
4 With damp palms break off marble-size pieces of meat
   and form into balls.
5 Heat the oil in a large saucepan and fry the meatballs, a
   few at a time, until they are browned on all sides.
6 Remove the meatballs and drain on kitchen paper.
7 Make the sauce by frying the onion in the oil remaining
   in the saucepan until it is lightly browned.
8 Add the garlic, tomatoes, water, salt and allspice and
   mix well.
9 Bring to the boil and cook for about 10 minutes, stirring
   occasionally.
10 Mash the tomato pieces as much as possible and then add
   the lemon juice, meatballs and cherries, if using fresh
   ones.
11 Simmer for 20–30 minutes until the meatballs are tender.
12 If using tinned cherries add them 5 minutes before the
   end of the cooking time.
13 To serve, either lightly toast one pita bread per person
   and spoon some of the meatballs and sauce over the top,
   or serve on a bed of rice pilav.

6–8 servings

YAH HABIB FEISAL
Liver kebab

> 450 g (1 lb) calf's liver
> 100 g (¼ lb) beef fat, cut into 10–12 pieces
> ½ teaspoon cumin
> ½ teaspoon black pepper
> ½ teaspoon paprika
> ½ teaspoon salt
> 225 g (½ lb) pickling onions, peeled
> *Garnish*
> 2 tablespoons finely chopped parsley
> Lemon wedges

1 Cut the liver into about 20 cubes.
2 Mix all the spices in a large bowl, add the liver and fat pieces and turn until they are well coated with the spices.
3 Leave for 30 minutes and then place 5 pieces of liver on to each skewer alternating with 2–3 onions and 2–3 pieces of fat.
4 Grill slowly over charcoal for 10–12 minutes, turning regularly.
5 Serve with the garnishes and accompanied by spring onions, radishes etc.

4 servings

MILAQ MESHWI-BI-TOUM
Grilled liver and garlic

This is another liver kebab popular in Egypt.

The pieces of liver are first marinated for 1 hour before grilling in:

> 1 tablespoon salt
> 150 ml (¼ pint) olive oil
> 1 teaspoon black pepper

1 teaspoon dried mint
Juice of 1 lemon
3 cloves garlic, crushed

After cooking, the kebabs are served on a bed of Roz Shami
– plain rice (see page 182).

4 servings

On a silver table

Cast down your eyes, lift up your soul,
Dig spoons into the great sauce bowls
Eat roast and fried and boiled and grilled.
Eat jams and jellies, warmed and chilled.
Eat quails cooked golden to the minute.
Eat nut-fed lamb with raisins in it.
Who would the warm stout capon blame
Date-coloured with judicious flame
Because he could not sing or fly?

The golds of man are manifold
But Allah made this kebab's gold.
He made this purslane salad sup
The soul of olives from a cup;
He set these twin and ponderous fish
To lie on mint leaves in a dish . . .

'Arabian Nights' – from *Poetry of the Orient*

KHAROUF MAHSHI
Whole roast lamb

'The earth is a mother that never dies' – Arab saying.

Whole roast lamb is a festive, ceremonial repast in the
Middle East where it is prepared for parties, festivals and
family gatherings. The sacrifice of lamb is related to the
ancient Middle Eastern religions predating both Judaism
and Islam. On the 10th day of the last month of
the Muhammedan year – 'Eid-el-Kurban' – a young, fat

lamb is slaughtered. The eyes of the animal are blackened and the head turned towards Mecca. The words 'In the name of God' are chanted over and over again while the animal is slaughtered and carefully bled. The lamb is usually roasted on a spit and, true to pre-Islamic traditions, the meat is distributed to the poor and to passers-by.

Again in the tradition of pre-Islamic cultures, lambs are slaughtered on a child's birthday, after a death, at the start of a holy pilgrimage and, even more often, at the end of a pilgrimage.

Kharouf Mahshi is the ideal exotic dinner or centre piece for a buffet. A whole lamb is usually enough for 25–30 people. The lamb is rinsed inside and out and then wiped dry, then rubbed inside and out with salt and black pepper and sprinkled with onion juice.

There are three main methods of cooking a lamb:

1 *The 'tandir':* This is a traditional method where a shallow (0·5–1 m (2–3 ft)) pit is dug, measuring approximately 1 × 1·8 m (3 × 6 ft). A bed of wood or charcoal is laid in the pit. The lamb is laid on the glowing charcoal and the whole is covered with earth. The cooking process takes about 6 hours. The lamb is then removed, brushed to remove any soil clinging to the skin and then placed on a large serving tray. The meat should virtually drop off the bones. It is served on a bed of rice and often accompanied by roasted pine kernels, almonds and raisins.

2 *Spit roasting:* By far the most popular method in the past, this has now been superseded by oven roasting. However, spit roasting is quite spectacular and great fun.

Spit the lamb with a wooden or metal rod. The rod is then rested on supports rising about 0·5–0·6 m (1 ft 6 in– 2 ft) above the ground which is dug out to a depth of 15 cm (6 in) and filled with either wood or charcoal. The spit usually has a handle to ease the turning of the lamb. Baste regularly with oil while cooking.

3 *Oven roasting:* This is the most common method of cooking whole lamb nowadays. Put the lamb into a large, deep baking tray and place in an oven preheated to 180°C (350°F, Gas Mark 4). Cook for 2 hours at this temperature and then lower the heat to 140°C (275°F, Gas Mark 1) and cook for a further 2–3 hours. Baste regularly and turn at least once while cooking.

Kharouf should, by tradition, be a baby lamb – 6–7 kg (15–20 lb). These are quite difficult to obtain in Europe unless you can buy direct from the farmer when they are in season. You may also find that your butcher can get one for you if you give him a few days' notice. Below is a typical recipe for a 11–13 kg (25–30 lb) lamb which is usually much easier to obtain.

11–13 kg (25–30 lb) lamb
Salt
Black pepper
1 tablespoon ground ginger
Juice of at least 4 lemons
Stuffing
1·3–1·5 kg (3–3½ lb) rice, washed thoroughly and drained
3 onions, chopped
5 tablespoons oil
225 g (½ lb) pistachio nuts, chopped
225 g (½ lb) walnuts, chopped
225 g (½ lb) almonds, chopped
225 g (½ lb) raisins
Salt and pepper to taste
Garnish
Sprigs of parsley
Thinly sliced onions, cucumber, tomatoes, radishes etc.

1 Prepare the lamb as explained above and rub it inside and out with the seasonings.

2 Make the stuffing by first boiling the rice until tender.

3 Fry the onions in the heated oil until they are soft.

4 Stir the onions and oil into the rice.

5 Add the nuts to the rice pan and stir well.

6 Add salt and pepper to taste. Work on the basis of 1 tea-spoon of salt and ½ teaspoon black pepper to each 450 g (1 lb) of rice.

7 Spoon the mixture into the lamb cavity, pressing in as much as possible.

8 With a strong thread sew up the opening.

9 Tie the feet together as tightly as possible to make it easier to fit the lamb into the oven.

10 Place in an oven preheated to 180°C (350°F, Gas Mark 4) and cook for about 2 hours basting frequently with its own juices.

11 Now lower the heat to 140°C (275°F, Gas Mark 1) and continue cooking until the meat is very tender and nicely browned. Turn at least once during cooking time.

12 Remove the tray very carefully from the oven.

13 Very carefully lift the lamb on to a large serving tray, cut the thread and with a large spoon fluff out some of the stuffing.

14 Garnish with the sliced vegetables.

25–30 people

ROZ-BIL-HUMMUS
Rice with meat and chickpeas

This dish is sometimes called Roz-bil-Dffeen and under that name is extremely popular in Jordan and Iraq. In Syria and Lebanon it is better known by our title. However the Syrians do not use turmeric, but rather cinnamon and, of course, lamb is preferred to beef. A filling, peasant dish, wholesome and very tasty, it makes an excellent meal accompanied by a fresh salad.

There is an Iraqi dish similar to this where chestnuts are used instead of chickpeas – Maglub-bil-Abufarwa. Incidentally, the finest chestnuts are still grown in the Khorasan region of southern Iran and this is perhaps where the substitution of chestnuts for chickpeas took place.

75 g (3 oz) butter
12 pickling onions, peeled
900 g (2 lb) stewing steak, cut into 2·5 cm (1 in) cubes
100 g (4 oz) chickpeas, soaked overnight in cold water
300 ml ($\frac{1}{2}$ pint) beef stock
1 teaspoon salt
$\frac{1}{2}$ teaspoon black pepper
1 teaspoon cumin
$\frac{1}{2}$ teaspoon turmeric
$\frac{1}{2}$ teaspoon cinnamon (optional)
450 g (1 lb) rice washed thoroughly in cold water and
    drained

1 Melt the butter in a large saucepan, add the onions and pieces of meat and cook, stirring frequently, for about 10 minutes.
2 Add the chickpeas, stock and sufficient water to cover by about 2·5 cm (1 in).
3 Stir in the salt, pepper, cumin, turmeric and cinnamon if you are using it.
4 Bring to the boil, lower the heat, cover and simmer for about 1–1$\frac{1}{2}$ hours or until the meat and chickpeas are tender.
5 Ensuring that the mixture is completely covered by water, bring briskly to the boil.
6 Stir in the rice, cover again, reduce the heat and simmer for 15–20 minutes until the rice is tender and the liquid absorbed.
7 Spoon into a large dish and serve.

6–8 servings

Poultry Dishes

TABYEET	*Pot-roasted stuffed chicken*
SHISH TAOUK	*Chicken kebab*
DAJAJ MAHSHI	*Chicken with rice and pine kernel stuffing*
FOUDJA-AL-JADDAH	*Apples stuffed with chicken and nuts*
ASSAFEER AND HAMAAN MESHWI	*Grilled small birds and pigeons*
DAJAJ SOURYANI	*Chicken with yogourt*
MUGHREBIEH	*Lebanese cous-cous*
KAPSA	*Chicken with rice and raisins*

TABYEET
Pot-roasted stuffed chicken

This is an Iraqi dish with northern overtones, especially in
the use of the dry-rice crust which is also loved by the
Azerbaijanians and the people of the Caucasus. The word
'tabyeet' in Arabic means 'to stay' and this refers to the fact
that the chicken should be kept in the spices for as long as
possible before cooking. It is a sophisticated dish from the
times of Haroun-al-Rasheed.

1·75 kg (4 lb) oven-ready chicken, including giblets
1 teaspoon salt
½ teaspoon black pepper
½ teaspoon ground cinnamon
½ teaspoon ground cardamon
3–4 cloves, ground
Pinch turmeric
Pinch cumin
350 g (¾ lb) rice
300 ml (½ pint) chicken stock
2 large or 3 medium tomatoes, coarsely chopped
60 ml (2 fl oz) oil or 50 g (2 oz) ghee
1 onion, finely chopped
1 pint water

1 Remove the giblets and retain them.
2 Wash the chicken and pat dry with kitchen paper.
3 Mix half the salt and black pepper with the cinnamon,
  cardamon, cloves, turmeric and cumin.

4 Rub this mixture generously into the outside and inside of the chicken.

5 Cover and leave the chicken in the refrigerator overnight to absorb the spices.

6 Wash 100 g (4 oz) of the rice under cold, running water and, when clean, leave it to soak for 30 minutes in cold water.

7 Meanwhile finely chop the liver and heart.

8 Drain the rice and mix it, in a bowl, with the remaining salt and black pepper and stir in half of the chopped tomatoes and the chopped giblets.

9 Place this mixture in a small saucepan, add the chicken stock, bring to the boil and simmer until all the liquid has been absorbed.

10 Spoon this mixture into the chicken cavity and sew up the opening with thick thread or string.

11 In a large saucepan or casserole heat the oil or ghee and sauté the onion until it is golden brown.

12 Add the remaining tomatoes and 300 ml ($\frac{1}{2}$ pint) water, stir well and place the chicken in the pan.

13 Cook until most of the water has evaporated, turning a few times until the chicken has begun to brown.

14 Add a further 300 ml ($\frac{1}{2}$ pint) water, bring quickly to the boil and then simmer, turning occasionally, until the chicken is tender.

15 Meanwhile wash the remaining 225 g (8 oz) rice.

16 When the chicken is tender remove it from the pan to an ovenproof dish and place in the oven to keep warm.

17 Add the remaining rice to the juices in the pan and continue simmering until all the liquid has evaporated and the rice is tender.

18 Return the chicken to the pan and keep over a very low heat until the rice is very dry and a dark brown crust has formed over the base of the pan.

19 Serve in a large serving dish with the dry crust broken up

into smaller pieces and arranged around the edge of the
dish as a garnish.

4–6 servings

SHISH TAOUK
Chicken kebab

I first encountered Shish Taouk some years ago in Lebanon
where it appears to have become the local version of Kentucky Chicken – such is its popularity. As it has become com-
mercialized it has naturally lost much of its original flavour.
I remember I was served 6–8 pieces of chicken breast inside
a pita bread. The chicken tasted of chicken – no more and no
less.

This is an Ottoman dish, the name still bearing its Turkish
origins. Although I deprecate its commercialism, the dish
itself when properly marinated is very tasty, cheap and
simple to prepare. An accompaniment of rice or fresh salad
is ideal.

1 1·5 kg (3 lb) chicken
Marinade
1 clove garlic, crushed
½ teaspoon salt
¼ teaspoon black pepper
75 ml (2½ fl oz) olive oil
½ teaspoon cayenne pepper
¼ teaspoon cumin
1 tablespoon lemon juice
½ teaspoon tomato purée (optional)

1 Wash the chicken and dry thoroughly.
2 Remove the skin.
3 Cut the flesh off the chicken (it should weigh about 450 g
[1 lb]).
4 Mix all the marinade ingredients together in a large bowl.

5 Cut the chicken flesh into 1·5–2·5 cm (¾–1 in) cubes.
6 Place the chicken in the marinade, turn until all the pieces are well coated and leave for at least 2 hours.
7 Thread the pieces on to skewers and grill over charcoal or under a grill for about 10 minutes, turning frequently.

4 servings

DAJAJ MAHSHI
Chicken with rice and pine kernel stuffing

This dish is a Syrian speciality, but popular throughout the Middle East. There are several variations – indeed, a twelfth-century manuscript, Kitab al Wusla ilal Habib, notes over 500 recipes for chicken alone. Sometimes rice and meat are used and sometimes other vegetables, eg celery, tomatoes, potatoes and green peppers, but I believe a rice and pine kernel stuffing is the most exquisite and delicate of all the Middle Eastern stuffings.

1 × 1·75 kg (4 lb) chicken, with giblets
25 g (1 oz) butter
1 small onion, finely chopped
50 g (2 oz) pine kernels or coarsely chopped almonds
100 g (4 oz) rice, washed
300 ml (½ pint) water
1 tablespoon currants or sultanas
3 teaspoons salt
1 teaspoon black pepper
25 g (1 oz) butter, melted
150 ml (¼ pint) yogourt

1 Melt the butter in a large saucepan, add the onion and fry until golden brown.
2 Coarsely chop the giblets and add to the pan together with the pine kernels or almonds and cook gently for a further 3 minutes.

3 Stir in the rice and cook for 2–3 minutes, stirring constantly.

4 Add the water, currants or sultanas, 2 teaspoons of the salt and ½ teaspoon of the black pepper.

5 Bring to the boil, reduce the heat and simmer for about 30 minutes or until the water has been absorbed.

6 Remove the pan from the heat and stir in the melted butter.

7 Wash and dry the chicken and spoon the rice mixture into the cavity. Reserve any remaining stuffing to heat and serve with the cooked chicken.

8 Secure the opening with a skewer or large needle and thread.

9 Mix the yogourt with the remaining salt and pepper and brush this mixture over the chicken.

10 Cook in an oven preheated to 180°C (350°F, Gas Mark 4) for 1½–2 hours, basting occasionally with the yogourt mixture.

11 When ready to serve heat the remaining stuffing and serve with the chicken.

4–6 servings

FOUDJA-AL-JADDAH
Apples stuffed with chicken and nuts

This is an Arabic dish from Jeddah. However, I am convinced that it is not of local origin because it is far too complicated and rich, Arab food being basically simple. The generous use of spices, herbs, fruits etc suggest this to be of (a) North African or (b) Persian origin and, since Arabia was throughout its history more in touch with the Arabs of Baghdad who in fact were of Persian origin and imbued with Persian culture and since Jeddah is the starting place for the final part of the holy pilgrimage to Mecca, I suspect that this

recipe is, in part, a local adaptation of an Iranian dish –
Dolmeh Sib, stuffed apples.

    8 medium-sized cooking apples
    225 g (½ lb) cooked chicken flesh, minced or finely
      chopped
    1 teaspoon salt
    ½ teaspoon black pepper
    50 g (2 oz) breadcrumbs
    6 cloves
    50 g (2 oz) chopped nuts
    ¼ teaspoon turmeric
    75 g (3 oz) raisins
    ¼ teaspoon cinnamon
    ¼ teaspoon ginger
    Sugar
    50 g (2 oz) butter

1 Wash the apples, core them and scoop out enough flesh to
  make a hole about 2·5–3·5 cm (1–1½ in) in diameter.
2 In a small bowl mix the chicken with the salt, pepper and
  breadcrumbs.
3 Add the cloves, nuts, turmeric, raisins, cinnamon and
  ginger and mix thoroughly.
4 Now stuff the apples with this mixture, but do not press
  too hard.
5 Arrange the apples in a large ovenproof dish and add
  sufficient hot water to come about halfway up the apples.
6 Sprinkle some sugar on to each apple.
7 Cut the 50 g (2 oz) butter into 8 pieces and put one knob on
  top of each apple.
8 Bake the apples in an oven preheated to 180°C (350°F,
  Gas Mark 4) for 30–40 minutes. Take care not to overcook
  or the apples will split.
9 Serve immediately, with boiled rice.

4 servings

ASSAFEER AND HAMAAN MESHWI
Grilled small birds and pigeons

When we were children we used to go to the woods and shoot, with home-made catapults, assafeer (small birds) which were plucked, washed and grilled on makeshift kebab grills and then eaten most heartily. I always remember a popular song of those days:

> Ana Asfoura, Ana Asfoura . . .
> I am a little bird my heart in flame,
> Love and desire wings in flame.
> I am a little bird from the shores of the Nile,
> I am a little bird in love, true love . . .

I recall this song even today since it was the equivalent of a 'number one' at the time. The very air of my childhood seems to have been filled with little birds in love.

The following recipes then are for small birds and pigeons. I have included them more out of curiosity than anything else. This is because, although small birds (eg sparrow, thrush, lark) in Britain and America are most suitable, the killing and eating of them is not only illegal but also extremely distasteful to most people. However, in some Middle Eastern countries assafeer are highly prized and extremely popular. Out of curiosity therefore, and only for that reason –

1 Pluck and remove the entrails.
2 Wash thoroughly.
3 Cut off the beak and lower legs.
4 Rub salt and pepper all over the body.
5 Tuck the head into the body.
6 Thread on to skewers and grill over charcoal for about 10 minutes, turning frequently.
7 Squeeze a few drops of lemon juice over the bird and eat – bones and all.

The result is marvellous! Never mind, perhaps when you happen to be passing through the Orient you may pluck up courage and try.

As for hamaan – this is pigeon. The pigeons in Britain are not quite up to the standard of those of the Middle East and so you could use poussin instead.

1 Pluck and remove the entrails.
2 Wash thoroughly.
3 Rub with salt and pepper.
4 Thread on to skewers and grill over charcoal for 15–20 minutes.
5 Serve with lemon juice and parsley sprinkled over the top and accompanied by a fresh salad.

Pigeons, and poussins, can be marinated very successfully. The following amounts are sufficient for 4 birds.

An Egyptian marinade
150 ml (¼ pint) olive oil
2 teaspoons cumin
2 teaspoons coriander
Juice of 1 onion, or 1 onion very finely chopped
2 cloves garlic, finely chopped
1 teaspoon cayenne pepper

1 Mix all the above ingredients together in a large bowl.
2 Add the birds, turn them several times and leave for 1–2 hours.
3 Grill the birds over charcoal, turning and basting occasionally.

A marinade from Syria
150 ml (¼ pint) olive oil
Juice of 1 lemon
1 teaspoon salt
¾ teaspoon black pepper
2 bay leaves

1 Mix all the above ingredients together in a large bowl.
2 Add the birds, turn several times, and leave for 1–2 hours.
3 Grill the birds over charcoal, turning and basting occasionally.
4 Serve sprinkled with chopped chervil or parsley.

DAJAJ SOURYANI
Chicken with yogourt

This is an Assyrian favourite. The Assyrians, of course, were once the most powerful nation in the Middle East and, although today they are few in number, they still retain a great number of their traditions. It is often forgotten by those who merely glance at the pages of history that the modern Iraqis, Syrians and Jordanians were once called Assyrians, and while the Arabs were still wandering in the desert the Assyrians had built a mighty culture and, I am sure, a rich culinary tradition. This recipe will give you an idea of that sophisticated and intricate cuisine.

   1 1·5 kg (3 lb) chicken, cut into 8 serving pieces
   4 tablespoons butter or ghee
   1 onion, finely chopped
   1 green pepper, finely sliced
   600 ml (1 pint) chicken stock
   1 teaspoon salt
   ½ teaspoon black pepper
   2 tablespoons sumak powder
   2 tablespoons ground almonds
   300 ml (½ pint) yogourt
   1 teaspoon cayenne pepper
   1 teaspoon ground cumin

1 Melt the better or ghee in a large saucepan and fry the chicken pieces, turning frequently, until they are browned all over.

 2 Remove the chicken pieces from the pan to a large plate and keep warm.
 3 Add the onion and green pepper to the pan and sauté for a few minutes until the onion is soft.
 4 Stir in the stock, salt, pepper and sumak.
 5 Return the chicken pieces to the saucepan, cover, lower the heat and simmer for about 45 minutes or until the chicken is tender.
 6 Transfer the chicken pieces to a warm serving dish.
 7 Add a few tablespoons of water to the almonds and mix to a smooth paste.
 8 Add this paste to the juices in the pan and bring to the boil, stirring all the time.
 9 Turn off the heat, add the yogourt to the sauce and stir in well.
10 Pour the sauce over the chicken, sprinkle with the cayenne pepper and cumin and serve immediately.
11 Serve accompanied by a rice or burghul (another Assyrian favourite) pilav.

4 servings

MUGHREBIEH
Lebanese cous-cous

1·5–1·8 kg (3–4 lb) chicken, cut into 4 pieces
100 g (4 oz) butter
450 g (1 lb) rump of mutton, cut into large pieces
100 g (4 oz) chickpeas, soaked overnight, or use drained, tinned chickpeas
2 teaspoons salt
2 teaspoons cayenne pepper
1 teaspoon cinnamon
1 teaspoon paprika
1·75 litres (3 pints) boiling water
450 g (1 lb) small onions, peeled and left whole

450 g (1 lb) cous-cous
50 g (2 oz) melted butter

1 Melt the butter in a large frying pan.
2 Add the chicken pieces and fry until brown all over, turning occasionally.
3 Remove the chicken pieces to a large saucepan and fry the mutton pieces in the same way.
4 Place the mutton in the pan with the chicken.
5 Drain the chickpeas, place in the frying pan and cook for 3–5 minutes.
6 Remove the chickpeas with a slotted spoon and add to the chicken and meat.
7 Add half of the salt, cayenne pepper, cinnamon and paprika and all of the boiling water to the saucepan, bring to the boil and then simmer for about 45 minutes or until the meat and chickpeas are tender.
8 Meanwhile fry the whole onions in the butter remaining in the frying pan for 3–4 minutes.
9 When the ingredients in the saucepan are almost tender add the contents of the frying pan to the saucepan and continue to simmer until everything is cooked.
10 Meanwhile spread the cous-cous on a baking sheet and sprinkle with warm salted water.
11 Work lightly between the fingers so that each grain is separate, moistened and beginning to swell.
12 Leave the cous-cous to rest for 15 minutes.
13 Repeat 11 and 12 three times.
14 Mix the remaining half of the salt, cayenne pepper, cinnamon and paprika with the melted butter and stir it into the cous-cous until all the grains are coated.
15 Pour the cous-cous into the top of a 'couscousier', or into a double saucepan, or a colander which fits very tightly over a saucepan, then cover with a tight-fitting lid.
16 If using a couscousier then cook the meat and chickpeas in the lower part and steam the cous-cous in the top part.

If using a double saucepan or colander and saucepan then half fill the lower pan with water seasoned with the spices which are flavouring the stew.

17　Bring the liquid to the boil and then boil steadily for about 1 hour, stirring the cous-cous occasionally, until the grains are soft and tender.

18　About 15 minutes before serving pour the cous-cous into a shallow pan and add a few tablespoons of the stock, onions and chickpeas.

19　Place over a low heat and simmer, stirring continuously, for 10–15 minutes.

20　To serve spread the cous-cous over a large serving platter and place the pieces of chicken and meat over the top together with any remaining onions and chickpeas.

21　Serve the remaining sauce in a separate dish.

4–6 servings

KAPSA
Chicken with rice and raisins

This is a popular dish from Saudi Arabia. In Iraq they make a dish called Habeet which is the meat version of the above except that they use their favourite spice – turmeric – instead of the cinnamon and nutmeg. Kapsa is, perhaps, the most common dish among the Bedouins although meat is used more often than chicken. This recipe is also known as Kapsa Javani (Javanese Kapsa) suggesting its Far Eastern origins. It is very popular throughout Saudi Arabia, especially on the east coast and in Bahrain. Always accompany it with fresh tomatoes, cucumbers, lettuce leaves and diced carrots.

50 g (2 oz) ghee or butter
2 onions, finely chopped
1 1·5 kg (3 lb) chicken, cleaned and cut into 8 serving pieces

Salt
600 ml (1 pint) stock
225 g (½ lb) long-grain rice, washed and drained
¼ teaspoon cinnamon
¼ teaspoon nutmeg
¼ teaspoon cumin
3–4 tablespoons raisins
2 bay leaves
Garnish
Pinch of paprika

1 Melt the ghee or butter in a large saucepan and sauté the onions until soft.
2 Rub the chicken pieces with salt, add them to the pan and fry, turning frequently, until they are brown all over.
3 Add sufficient water just to cover and bring to the boil.
4 Cover the pan and simmer until the chicken pieces are tender.
5 Meanwhile place the rice in a bowl, cover with cold water and leave to soak for about 30 minutes.
6 When the chicken is cooked strain off the liquid into a measuring jug. To cook the rice you need 600 ml (1 pint) of stock and if there is not enough make it up by adding water.
7 Cover the chicken and keep warm.
8 Place the stock in a pan and bring quickly to the boil.
9 Drain the rice and add it to the pan.
10 Stir in ½ teaspoon salt, the cinnamon, nutmeg, cumin, raisins and bay leaves and simmer until all the moisture is absorbed and the rice is tender.
11 Arrange the rice around a large platter and pile the chicken and onions into the centre.
12 Sprinkle with the paprika and serve.

4 servings

Meat with Vegetables Dishes

LIFT YAKHNIT	*Turnip stew*
BASAL BADAWI	*Onions stuffed with meat, nuts, fruit and yogourt*
BAMIA	*Meat and okra stew*
SHEIK-EL-MAHSHI	*Courgettes filled with meat and nuts*
FASOULIYEH	*French bean stew*
BASAL MESHWI	*Stuffed onions*
MARGOG	*Meat and courgette stew*

LIFT YAKHNIT
Turnip stew

This is an Iraqi recipe. Turnips are very popular in Iraq with
turnip pickles – maayi – and this dish which is a rich stew of
turnips, meat, tomatoes and spices. It is simple to prepare
and wholesome, and is traditionally served with a rice pilav.

900 g (2 lb) shoulder of lamb, cut into 5 cm (2 in) pieces
6 large turnips, peeled and cut into 5 cm (2 in) pieces
4 tomatoes, coarsely chopped
1 tablespoon tomato purée
1 teaspoon salt
½ teaspoon turmeric
½ teaspoon black pepper
½ teaspoon sweet basil
½ teaspoon oregano
Juice of 1 lemon

1 Place the pieces of lamb in a large saucepan, add sufficient
   water to cover by about 2·5 cm (1 in), cover the pan and
   simmer until the meat is tender – about 1 hour.
2 Remove the pieces of lamb and reserve the stock. You will
   need about 600 ml (1 pint) of stock, so make up with water
   if there is not enough.
3 Meanwhile cook the turnips, with just sufficient water to
   cover, until tender. Add a little more water if necessary.
4 Add the meat, tomatoes, tomato purée, salt, turmeric,
   black pepper, basil, oregano and lemon juice to the
   turnips and their remaining liquid.
5 Mix well and add the stock.

6 Cover the pan and simmer over a low heat for about ½ hour or until the flavours are well blended.
7 Serve in a large dish with a rice pilav.

6 servings

BASAL BADAWI
Onions stuffed with meat, nuts, fruit and yogourt

'He who introduces himself between the onion and the peel, does not go forth without its strong smell' – Egyptian proverb.

As the name suggests this is a Bedouin dish and it comes from Jordan. It is one of the traditional dishes of the nomadic people. Nevertheless it is a rather sophisticated dish that usually makes its appearance on feast days, at celebrations etc. Accompany with fresh vegetables, eg radishes, tomatoes, sliced cucumber, or with a pilav of your choice, eg Roz Ahmar. The saffron rice will give the entire dish a pure beauty worthy of the 'guardians of the desert'.

    4 large onions
    100 g (4 oz) minced meat
    ½ teaspoon salt
    Pinch of black pepper
    150 ml (¼ pint) yogourt
    2 tablespoons finely chopped dates
    2 tablespoons coarsely chopped walnuts
    1 tablespoon raisins or sultanas
    4 tablespoons buttered breadcrumbs
    Garnish
    Small sprigs parsley
    Sliced radishes

1 Skin the onions.
2 Half fill a large saucepan with slightly salted water, bring to the boil, add the onions and simmer for about 15 minutes or until the onions are fairly tender.

3 Drain the onions and allow to cool.

4 Cut thin slices from the root end of each onion and
   remove each centre leaving an outer shell about 1·5 cm
   (³/₄ in) thick. Set aside.

5 In a small bowl mix together the meat, salt, pepper,
   yogourt, dates, walnuts, raisins and half the breadcrumbs.

6 Spoon this mixture into the onions and press down quite
   firmly.

7 Top each onion with the remainder of the buttered
   breadcrumbs.

8 Arrange the onions in a casserole dish.

9 Place in an oven preheated to 180°C (350°F, Gas Mark 4)
   and cook for about 1 hour or until the meat is well
   cooked.

10 Serve immediately, garnished with the parsley and
   radishes.

4 servings

BAMIA
Meat and okra stew

Bamia or okra, sometimes better known as ladies' fingers, is
a favourite vegetable of Middle Eastern cooks. Originally
from India it is particularly popular in Turkey, Egypt and
especially Iraq where it is regarded as a national dish. There
are many versions of this dish, this one being from Iraq.

   Always use fresh okra if you possibly can – especially if you
wish to create the decorative pattern suggested in this recipe.
If it is impossible to find fresh okra then a tinned version will
do, but you will be unable to create the decoration suggested
and must cook the okra and meat together. Note also that
the meat should be almost cooked before you add the tinned
okra as the tinned vegetable disintegrates if cooked for very
long.

This is a simple and visually attractive recipe. I have seen accomplished cooks cover the casserole with a large plate and swiftly turn the dish over without damaging the arrangement. I am not sure I should encourage you to try this! It is traditionally served with a rice pilav.

675 g (1½ lb) okra
450 g (1 lb) lamb, cut into 1 cm (½ in) pieces
Oil for frying
225 g (½ lb) tomatoes, as ripe as possible or, preferably, tinned
1 teaspoon salt
1 tablespoon lemon juice
½ teaspoon black pepper
¼ teaspoon allspice

1 Wash the okra, dry thoroughly and cut off the hard stems.
2 Heat some oil in a large saucepan and gently fry the okra for a few minutes.
3 Remove the okra, drain on kitchen paper and leave to cool a little.
4 Now arrange the okra individually around the edge of a shallow casserole dish. You do this by placing them pointed ends alternately inwards and outwards.
5 Once the first layer is thus arranged place a second layer on top contrariwise, thus the vegetables will be intertwined and tightly held. Continue in this way until all the vegetables are used up.
6 There should be a well in the centre of the casserole. Fill this with the pieces of meat.
7 Meanwhile, if using fresh tomatoes, cook them with very little water and squash them until reduced to a pulp.
8 Now rub the tomatoes, fresh or tinned, through a sieve into a small bowl.
9 Add the salt, lemon juice, pepper and allspice to the tomato paste and mix well.

10 Pour the tomato mixture all over the vegetables and meat.

11 Cover the casserole, place in an oven preheated to 170°C (325°F, Gas Mark 3) and cook for 45–50 minutes or until the meat is tender and the okra soft, but not mushy.

4–6 servings

SHEIK-EL-MAHSHI
Courgettes filled with meat and nuts

Literally translated this dish means 'the King of all stuffed dishes', for it contains meat and nuts only, and meat was (and still is) very expensive. A Syrian speciality, also popular with Cilician Armenians. In some areas aubergines are used instead of courgettes.

Although 'stuffed' vegetable dishes are known amongst the Arab people, they are not as widespread as they are amongst the Armenians and Turks of Eastern Anatolia. The principle of drying vegetables for later use is very old but basically is that of people who farmed and cultivated and certainly not of nomadic tribes.

12 small courgettes (if not available then use 8 medium-sized ones)
Cooking oil
Stuffing
450 g (1 lb) minced lamb
1 small onion, finely chopped
1 tablespoon tomato purée
100 g (4 oz) pine kernels or chopped walnuts
2 tablespoons chopped parsley
1 teaspoon salt
½ teaspoon black pepper
1 teaspoon allspice
Sauce
25 g (1 oz) butter
1 clove garlic, crushed

1 tablespoon tomato purée
600 ml (1 pint) water
1 teaspoon salt
½ teaspoon black pepper

1 Cover the base of a large frying pan with about 1 cm (½ in) cooking oil.
2 Slice the stalk ends off the courgettes.
3 Remove as much of the flesh as possible from each courgette using an apple corer. Ideally the shell should be about 5 mm (¼ in) thick. Take care not to split, or to make holes in, the shell.
4 Wash the courgettes under cold running water and then dry with kitchen paper.
5 Heat the oil in the frying pan, add the courgettes a few at a time and fry gently for about 10 minutes, turning from time to time.
6 When cooked set aside on kitchen paper to drain and cool.
7 To make the filling, place the meat and onion in a saucepan and cook over a moderate heat for 20–30 minutes, stirring frequently to prevent sticking.
8 Stir in the remaining filling ingredients and cook for about another 10 minutes.
9 Preheat the oven to 200°C (400°F, Gas Mark 6).
10 Spoon the meat mixture into the courgettes.
11 Lay the vegetables side by side in an ovenproof dish.
12 To make the sauce, first heat the butter in a saucepan.
13 Add the garlic and tomato purée and cook, stirring occasionally, for 3–4 minutes.
14 Add the water, salt and pepper, bring to the boil and pour into the dish.
15 Place the dish in the oven and cook for about 20 minutes.
16 Serve with fresh salad and plain rice pilav.

4 servings

FASOULIYEH
French bean stew

French beans are popular throughout the Middle East and this dish appears in all the ethnic cuisines of the area. The Greeks, Turks and Armenians, as well as the Arabs, make several dishes with this vegetable. The recipe below is Syrian and differs from most Arab stews in that it is related to the Ottoman cuisine and hence to the Turkish-Armenian one. Traditionally accompanied by a rice pilav, you can also eat fasouliyeh with bread or boiled potatoes.

25 g (1 oz) butter
675 g (1½ lb) shoulder of lamb, cut into 2·5 cm (1 in) cubes
1 large onion, thickly sliced
2 cloves garlic, crushed
2 tablespoons tomato purée
1 tablespoon salt
1 teaspoon black pepper
½ teaspoon chilli powder
1 teaspoon allspice
675 g (1½ lb) french beans
4 tomatoes, coarsely chopped
600 ml (1 pint) water
1–2 tablespoons lemon juice (optional)

1 Heat the butter in a large saucepan and sauté the meat, onion and garlic until the onion is soft and the meat is sealed.
2 Add the tomato purée, salt, black pepper, chilli powder and allspice and cook for 5 minutes, stirring frequently.
3 Stir in the french beans and tomatoes and water and bring to the boil.
4 Cover and cook for about 1 hour or until the meat is tender, stirring occasionally.
5 Ten minutes before serving stir in the lemon juice and simmer.
6 Serve with chosen accompaniment.

4–6 servings

BASAL MESHWI
Stuffed onions

'What can I think of the good qualities of onion as every bite draws tears?' – Arab proverb.

This is a speciality from Mecca, the Holy City of Islam. Stuffed vegetables are popular throughout the Middle East and especially in Turkey, Armenia and Syria. In general they are not an Arab speciality and, where they do appear, as with this recipe, they are an acquisition from another nation. Mecca and Medina are, of course, still the only places in Saudi Arabia where throughout the ages Muslims have immigrated rather than emigrated.

2 large onions
50 g (2 oz) ghee or butter
Water
2 tablespoons lemon or lime juice
Stuffing
225 g (½ lb) lean beef, minced
75 g (3 oz) rice, washed thoroughly and drained
2 tablespoons finely chopped parsley
1 teaspoon salt
½ teaspoon black pepper
½ teaspoon allspice

1 Peel the onions.
2 With a sharp knife make a cut in each one from top to bottom, on one side, into the centre.
3 Half fill a large saucepan with boiling water, add the onions and simmer for about 45 minutes or until each layer of the onion can easily be detached.
4 Drain and leave until cool enough to handle.
5 Meanwhile put all the stuffing ingredients together in a large bowl and knead thoroughly with damp palms until smooth and well blended.
6 Carefully separate each onion layer.

7 Put 1 tablespoon of the stuffing into the hollow of each onion layer. A little more may be necessary in the large layers and a little less in the smaller layers.

8 Roll each layer up tightly and tie with a piece of thread.

9 Repeat until all the layers are filled and secured.

10 Melt the butter in a frying pan and sauté a few onion rolls at a time turning occasionally until they are a light golden colour.

11 When they are all sautéed arrange them tightly in a shallow ovenproof dish.

12 Add enough boiling water to cover by 1 cm (½ in), sprinkle over the lemon or lime juice and cover.

13 Place in an oven preheated to 180°C (350°F, Gas Mark 4) and cook for about 50–60 minutes or until the meat is cooked.

14 Serve with fresh salad or boiled potatoes.

4 servings

MARGOG
Meat and courgette stew

A classic Bedouin dish from Arabia which, with Kapsa, Saalik and Kharouf Mahshi, is one of the most popular dishes served in an Arab menzil (camp). It is tasty, filling and simple to make – as are all Bedouin dishes. This dish is traditionally served on a bed of rice and always accompanied by fresh fruits, eg apples, oranges, bananas.

5–6 tablespoons oil
1 onion, thinly sliced
675 g (1½ lb) shoulder of lamb, cut into 2·5 cm (1 in) cubes
1 teaspoon salt
½ teaspoon black pepper
½ teaspoon chilli powder
½ teaspoon cardamon powder
3 courgettes, cut crossways into 1 cm (½ in) slices

3 tomatoes, coarsely chopped
300 ml (½ pint) beef stock or water
Dough
100 g (4 oz) self-raising flour
1 teaspoon salt
1 teaspoon sugar
Water

1 Heat the oil in a large saucepan and sauté the onion until soft.
2 Add the meat and fry for a few more minutes, turning frequently until nicely browned.
3 Add the salt, black pepper, chilli powder and ground cardamon, mix thoroughly and continue frying for a further 10 minutes. Remove from the heat.
4 Add the courgettes, tomatoes and stock or water and stir until well mixed.
5 Turn this mixture into a large ovenproof casserole and bring to the boil over a moderate heat.
6 Place in an oven preheated to 190°C (375°F, Gas Mark 5) and cook for about 1 hour or until the meat is tender.
7 Meanwhile to make the dough, first place the sifted flour, salt and sugar in a mixing bowl.
8 Add some cold water, a little at a time, and knead until the dough becomes smooth and firm.
9 Flour a working surface and rolling pin and roll the dough out until it is 5 mm (¼ in) thick.
10 Cut the dough into 2·5 cm (1 in) square pieces.
11 After the casserole has been in the oven for 15 minutes remove it and lay the squares of dough over the surface.
12 Cover, return to the oven and continue cooking until the meat is tender.
13 Serve as suggested above.

4–6 servings

Fish Dishes

SAYYADIAH	*Fish with rice*
SAMAK MAQLI	*Fried fish*
COUSBAREIAH SAUCE	*Rich fish sauce*
SAMAK MESHWI	*Fish grilled over charcoal*
SAMAK-BI-TAHINA	*Fish with tahina sauce*
SAMAK KAMOUNIEH	*Baked fish with cumin*
SAMAK HARRAH	*Fish stuffed with walnuts and pomegranate seeds*
BARGHOON EL-BAHAR BIL ROZ	*Shrimp fried rice*
SALONA	*Fried fish with tomatoes*

SAYYADIAH
Fish with rice

There are several variations of this dish which is, basically, fish cooked with rice. Sometimes the rice and fish are cooked separately, but often they are cooked together like a stew, as below. Among the peasants of Egypt this dish is popular as a soup.

This recipe is a fish casserole with the saffron giving the rice a bright yellow colour. It is an old family favourite from Syria.

    2 tablespoons butter
    900 g (2 lb) halibut steaks, each cut into halves
    2 tablespoons lemon juice
    ½ teaspoon salt
    ¼ teaspoon black pepper
    2 tablespoons chopped parsley
Stew
    6 tablespoons olive oil
    1 onion, finely chopped
    2 tablespoons pine kernels
    1 tablespoon sultanas or raisins
    ½ teaspoon allspice
    Roz Ahmar – saffron rice (see page 182). See chapter on rice dishes and use quantities as for Roz Shami (page 182)
    2 tablespoons lemon juice
    2 tablespoons chopped parsley
    1 teaspoon salt
    ½ teaspoon black pepper

Sauce

4 tablespoons olive oil
1 tablespoon pine kernels
1 tablespoon dried mint
1 tablespoon lemon juice
½ teaspoon cumin

1 Melt half the butter in a large shallow baking dish and add the pieces of fish.
2 Sprinkle with the lemon juice, salt, pepper and chopped parsley.
3 Dot the remaining butter over the fish.
4 Place in an oven preheated to 170°C (325°F, Gas Mark 3) and cook until the fish flakes easily.
5 Remove from the oven, leave to cool and then flake the fish and remove and discard the bones.
6 Set the fish aside.
7 Heat the oil in a large saucepan and sauté the onions until soft.
8 Add the nuts, raisins, allspice and Roz Ahmar.
9 Add the lemon juice, parsley, salt and pepper and mix well.
10 Now spread half of this mixture over the base of a large shallow baking dish.
11 Spread half of the reserved fish over the top.
12 Repeat the layer of rice mixture and top this with the remaining fish.
13 To prepare the sauce, first heat the oil in a small frying pan.
14 Add the nuts, mint, cumin and lemon juice and sauté for 5 minutes, stirring frequently.
15 Pour the sauce evenly over the surface of the casserole.
16 Place in an oven preheated to 180°C (350°F, Gas Mark 4) and bake for approximately 15 minutes or until the ingredients are heated through.
17 Serve with a bowl of fresh salad.

6 servings

SAMAK MAQLI
Fried fish

'Throw him into the river and he will rise with a fish in his mouth' – refers to lucky people.

By far the most popular way of cooking fish in the Middle East is by frying it in oil. The Arabs, in particular, are very fond of this method. The fish, often straight from the sea, is deep fried and served either with lemon wedges, with a Tartare sauce or, as in the Beirut restaurants, with a bowl of fresh salad. The famous Lebanese fish, Sultan Ibrahim (red mullet), is usually served thus and it is quite an experience to sit in one of the many fish restaurants of Beirut and see how kilos (literally) of fried fish are consumed. Incidentally, one does not order a fish or two, but a kilo or two which is always accompanied by fresh vegetables, eg small cucumbers, tomatoes, lettuce, pickled aubergines, fresh tarragon, spring onions, lemons etc.

Generally speaking however, the Arabs are not great fish eaters – certainly not the Iraqis or the mass of the Egyptians, Syrians and Jordanians. When they do, it is either fried or charcoal-grilled – simple and tasty perhaps, but not gastronomically exciting.

This is a typical recipe for frying. I have coupled it with a delicious Egyptian sauce called Cousbareiah, made with hazelnuts, walnuts and pine kernels and which, I find, gives an added zest to the fish dish.

> 900 g (2 lb) fish, washed and cleaned. If the fish are small (eg sprats or whitebait) then leave them whole, otherwise cut larger ones (eg mullet, bream, bass, turbot, cod, etc) into thick slices
> Flour
> Oil for deep frying, preferably olive, but nut oil will do

1 In a deep pan heat sufficient oil to cover the fish while frying.

2 Dry the fish on kitchen paper and then dredge with flour.
3 Fry a few pieces of the fish at a time. Do not let the temperature of the oil drop or the fish will not be crisp.
4 Cook for 5–10 minutes, shaking the pan occasionally to prevent sticking.
5 Serve with the accompaniments suggested above.

4–6 servings

COUSBAREIAH SAUCE
Rich Fish Sauce

900 g (2 lb) fish, prepared as for fried fish
2 tablespoons oil
1 onion, thinly sliced
2 tomatoes, thinly sliced
50 g (2 oz) hazelnuts, chopped
50 g (2 oz) walnuts, chopped
50 g (2 oz) pine kernels
½ teaspoon allspice
1 teaspoon salt
½ teaspoon black pepper
2 tablespoons finely chopped parsley

1 Heat the oil in a pan and sauté the onions until golden brown.
2 Add the tomatoes and all the nuts and fry for 2–3 minutes, stirring constantly.
3 Add 60 ml (2 fl oz) water, the allspice, salt and pepper and parsley and simmer for about 5 minutes.
4 Either place the pieces of raw fish carefully in the sauce and cook gently for about 15 minutes over a low heat basting occasionally, or place the pieces of fish in an oven-proof dish, pour the sauce over the top and bake in an oven preheated to 200°C (400°F, Gas Mark 6) for about 15–20 minutes.
5 Serve with a plain rice pilav or a fresh salad.

4–6 servings

SAMAK MESHWI
Fish grilled over charcoal

'Handling fish is like handling people. They both need patience, care and careful management – otherwise the end product is bad' – Arab wisdom.

Fish has always been an important source of protein for man, and the warm waters of the Mediterranean contain many excellent fish. However, fish dishes are only found near the coast, also by tradition most Middle Eastern people are not fish eaters but are lovers of lamb, mutton and goat – a by-product of their nomadic origins.

One excellent way of eating fish is grilled over a charcoal fire. All types and sizes of fish can be successfully cooked in this way. The simplest method is to wash, clean and scale the fish and lightly sprinkle with salt. Lightly oil a skewer or double grill and then proceed to cook the fish. However, there are many marinades which will enhance the flavour of the fish, and I give here two excellent Arab examples.

900 g (2 lb) fish, eg bass, bream, halibut, red mullet etc. If the fish are small allow one per person, otherwise cut into steaks

Marinade 1
75 ml ($\frac{1}{8}$ pint) olive oil
1 tablespoon salt
1 teaspoon black pepper
$\frac{1}{2}$ teaspoon allspice
2 tablespoons lemon juice

Marinade 2
1 onion, cut into 5 mm ($\frac{1}{4}$ in) slices and separated into rings
2 tablespoons lemon juice
3 tablespoons olive oil
1 tablespoon salt
$\frac{1}{2}$ teaspoon black pepper

1 clove garlic, finely chopped
1 teaspoon cumin powder
4 bay leaves
Garnish
Chopped parsley
Lemon wedges

1 Clean and wash the fish and pat dry on kitchen paper.
2 Mix the marinade of your choice in a shallow dish.
3 Add the fish, turn them in the marinade to coat them all over and set aside for about 2 hours.
4 Place the fish in a lightly oiled double grill or on to skewers.
5 Cook over charcoal, turning every 2 or 3 minutes and basting regularly with the marinade.
6 The average cooking time is about 15–20 minutes, but it depends to a certain extent on the size of the fish. Test with a fork – if the flesh flakes easily then it is cooked.
7 Transfer to a large plate, garnish and serve immediately.

4 servings

SAMAK-BI-TAHINA
Fish with tahina sauce

This is one of the most popular fish dishes in Syria and Lebanon. The fish is cooked in the oven and the sauce is prepared separately, to be poured over the fish when cold. Serve with pita bread or a salad of your choice.

1 large 1·5 kg (3 lb) fish, or the equivalent weight in small fish
Oil
Salt
Sauce
2 cloves garlic
1 teaspoon salt

10 tablespoons tahina paste
6 tablespoons water
Juice of 1 lemon
3 tablespoons parsley, finely chopped
Garnish
1 pomegranate, seeded

1 Wash the fish thoroughly.
2 Rub with salt inside and out and set aside for 1 hour.
3 Brush the fish thoroughly with oil, place in a well-greased
   dish and bake in an oven preheated to 200°C (400°F, Gas
   Mark 6) for about 30 minutes or until the flesh flakes
   easily with a fork.
4 Remove from the oven, transfer to a serving dish and set
   aside to cool.
5 To prepare the sauce, first pound the garlic together with
   the salt.
6 Stir in the tahina and then mix in the water and lemon
   juice and beat for 5 minutes.
7 Mix in the parsley.
8 Pour the sauce over the fish, sprinkle with the pomegranate seeds and serve.

6 servings

SAMAK KAMOUNIEH
Baked fish with cumin

This is an Egyptian speciality with a strong oriental flavour
about it through the use of cumin powder. It is a simple and
wholesome meal which is traditionally served with plain rice.
Sometimes other vegetables are used in the making of the
sauce, such as celery or leeks.

   4 × 225 g (½ lb) steaks of white fish, eg cod, bream, bass or
      haddock
   5 tablespoons oil

1 large onion, thinly sliced
2 cloves garlic, thinly sliced
1 tablespoon cumin
2 tablespoons tomato purée
1 teaspoon salt
¼ teaspoon black pepper
300 ml (½ pint) water
1 tomato, thinly sliced

1 Heat 4 tablespoons of the oil in a saucepan, add the onions, garlic and cumin and fry for about 5 minutes until the onions are soft and golden brown.
2 Stir in the tomato purée, ½ teaspoon of the salt, the black pepper and the water and cook for a further 5 minutes until most of the water has evaporated and the mixture has thickened.
3 Wash and dry the fish.
4 Brush a shallow ovenproof dish with a little oil.
5 Arrange the steaks, side by side, in the dish.
6 Sprinkle the fish with the remaining salt.
7 Now pour the tomato-based sauce over the fish.
8 Arrange the tomato slices over the top and sprinkle with the remaining oil.
9 Cover the dish, place in an oven preheated to 180°C (350°F, Gas Mark 4) and bake for about 40 minutes. Remove after half the cooking time and check the liquid. If most of it has evaporated then add a few more tablespoons of water.
10 For the last half of the cooking time remove the cover so that the tomatoes become lightly browned and the sauce bubbly.

4 servings

POMEGRANATES

There was once a man who had many pomegranates in his orchard and for many an autumn he would put his pomegranates on silver trays outside his dwelling, and upon the trays he would place signs upon which he himself had written 'Take out for aught. You are welcome.' But people passed by and no one took the fruit. Then the man bethought him, and one autumn he placed no pomegranates on silver trays outside of his dwelling, but he raised his sign in large lettering: 'Here we have the best pomegranates in the land, but we sell them for more silver than any other pomegranates.' And now behold, all the men and women of the neighbourhood came rushing to buy.

K. Gibran (Arab philosopher) – 'The Wanderer'

SAMAK HARRAH
Fish stuffed with walnuts and pomegranate seeds

'What thing lives always in prison and dies when it breathes the free air? – Fish' –Egyptian saying.

A festive dish for that special occasion, this is a Syrian speciality but it is popular also in Egypt, Lebanon and Jordan. It is a sophisticated recipe most probably of Ottoman origin since most Arab fish dishes are much simpler. It is an exceptionally attractive dish with the red of the pomegranates contrasting with the black olives and the green of the pistachio nuts creating the colours of an oriental carpet.

This dish is often accompanied by a bowl of tarator – that ever-popular Syrian-Lebanese dip. I personally prefer to do without this since I find the delicate flavour of the fish is lost when the garlic-based tarator is applied.

1·5–1·75 kg (3–4 lb) whole sea bass or bream
2 teaspoons salt
Olive oil
1 onion, finely chopped
1 green pepper, finely chopped
3 tablespoons finely chopped walnuts
5 tablespoons finely chopped parsley
1 pomegranate, seeds removed, separated and retained
1 teaspoon black pepper

Garnish
Lettuce leaves
1 lemon, cut into wedges
4–5 radishes, thinly sliced
8–10 black olives
1 teaspoon pine kernels or pistachio nuts, coarsely
   chopped

1 Wash the fish under cold running water then clean and
   scale it, remove the eyes but leave the head and tail on.
2 Sprinkle inside and out with 1 teaspoon of the salt.
3 Pour 3 tablespoons of the oil into a shallow baking dish.
4 Lay the fish in the dish, pour another 2 tablespoons of the
   oil over the fish and leave for about ½ hour.
5 Meanwhile, heat 4–5 tablespoons of olive oil in a frying
   pan and sauté the onion until soft and golden brown.
6 Stir in the green pepper and walnuts, cook for 5 minutes
   and remove from the heat.
7 Add 4 tablespoons of the parsley, half the pomegranate
   seeds, the remaining salt and the black pepper and mix
   thoroughly.
8 Fill the fish with this stuffing and close the opening with
   a small skewer.
9 Bake the fish in an oven preheated to 180°C (350°F, Gas
   Mark 4) for about 1 hour basting occasionally with its
   own juices.
10 Serve the fish on a large platter on a bed of lettuce leaves.
11 Decorate with the lemon wedges, sliced radishes and
   black olives.
12 Sprinkle with the nuts and the remaining pomegranate
   seeds and parsley.

6 servings

BARGHOON EL-BAHAR BIL ROZ
Shrimp fried rice

Shrimps and prawns are found in abundance along the
eastern coastline of Saudi Arabia and therefore rice and
shrimp dishes are very popular throughout this region. The

Kuwaitis like their rice and shrimps fried together with egg, soy sauce and pineapple slices while in Bahrain they like to marinate the shrimps and then fry them in oil. They are also very fond of curry dishes and make an excellent curried shrimp in tomato sauce.

Curry powder, soy sauce, pineapples etc are all the by-products of the centuries-old trade between the Arab Gulf and the Indian sub-continent. There is also the fact that a great number of the 'Arabs' in these regions are of Indian and Javanese origins.

> Roz Ahmar – saffron rice (see page 182)
> 3 tablespoons vegetable oil
> 1 stick celery, cut into 1 cm ($\frac{1}{2}$ in) pieces
> 100 g (4 oz) french beans, cut into 5 cm (2 in) pieces
> 4 spring onions, thinly sliced
> 2 tablespoons soy sauce
> 450 g (1 lb) shrimps (frozen will do as well as fresh)
> 2 eggs
> 2 tablespoons blanched almonds

1 Prepare the Roz Ahmar according to its recipe and keep warm.
2 Heat the oil in a large saucepan and fry the celery, french beans and half the spring onions for 3–4 minutes, stirring all the time.
3 Add the soy sauce and the shrimps and continue stirring gently for a few minutes.
4 Break the eggs into a small bowl, lightly beat and then add to the pan.
5 Lower the heat and continue stirring the mixture until the eggs are cooked.
6 Meanwhile, under a grill, cook the almonds for a few minutes until golden brown.
7 Transfer the Roz Ahmar to a large serving plate and top with the shrimps and vegetables.
8 Garnish with the remaining spring onions and sprinkle with the toasted almonds.

4–6 servings

SALONA
Fried fish with tomatoes

This is an Iraqi dish very popular in the south of the country. There is more than a hint of the Indian sub-continent in this recipe, especially with the inclusion of curry powder and turmeric. Iraq is not very rich in fish dishes and apart from the famed Masgoof, there are few interesting ones most of which almost always include curry powder, turmeric, ginger, soy sauce etc, suggesting a strong Far-Eastern influence.

    4 fish fillets
    Oil for frying
    2 onions, coarsely chopped
    1 tablespoon curry powder
    ½ teaspoon turmeric
    1½ teaspoons salt
    ½ teaspoon black pepper
    ½ teaspoon paprika
    Water
    4 tomatoes, sliced

1 Wash the fish and dry on kitchen paper.
2 Heat the oil in a large frying pan and fry the fish until lightly browned, about 5–7 minutes.
3 Remove the fish and arrange them in an ovenproof dish.
4 In the same oil sauté the onions until lightly browned.
5 Remove them, drain and arrange over the fish.
6 Sprinkle the curry powder, turmeric, 1 teaspoon of the salt, pepper and paprika over the onions and fish.
7 Add just enough water to cover.
8 Arrange the sliced tomatoes over the top and sprinkle with the remaining salt.
9 Cover, place in an oven preheated to 190°C (375°F, Gas Mark 5) and cook for 15 minutes.
10 Lower the heat to 170°C (325°F, Gas Mark 3), uncover the fish and cook for a further 15 minutes or until much of the water has evaporated.
11 Serve with a rice pilav of your choice and a fresh salad.

4 servings

Rice Dishes

ROZ	*Plain rice pilav*
ROZ AHMAR	*Red rice*
ROZ SHAMI	*Damascus rice*
ROZ-OU-HAMOUD	*Rice with sauce*
ROZ-BIL-SHAGHRIEH	*Rice with vermicelli*
ROZ-BIL-TAMAR	*Rice with almonds and dates*
KITRY	*Rice and lentil pilav*
ROZ-BIL-BETINGAN	*Rice and aubergine pilav*
MUJADDARAH	*Rice and lentils*

ROZ
Rice

Rice is a basic dish over most of the Middle East except in North Africa where cous-cous is used and in Eastern Turkey and Northern Iraq where Burghul is more popular.

Rice is always present on the dinner table in one form or another. However, unlike the Iranians, Azerbaijanians, Armenians or Turks, the Arab rice dishes are limited in imagination and there is hardly a recipe – unless influenced by the above nations – that explores the tremendous potentialities of rice.

There are many ways of cooking rice, but they can be narrowed down to three basic methods.

1 Rice fried in butter and then boiled in water or stock and seasoned with salt and often other spices. This is Roz – plain rice pilav.
2 Rice boiled in water with a pinch of salt. This is Roz Shami – Damascus rice.
3 Steamed rice. This is a Persian method.

It is easier to cook rice by volume, ie for 1 teacup (175 g [6 oz]) rice use 2 teacups (475 ml [16 fl oz]) water. For every further one teacup (175 g [6 oz]) rice use 1½ teacups (350 ml [12 fl oz]) water.

ROZ
Plain rice Pilav

    50 g (2 oz) butter

 350 g (12 oz [2 teacups]) long-grain rice, washed
  thoroughly under cold running water and drained
 1 teaspoon salt
 850 ml (28 fl oz [3½ teacups]) stock or water, boiling

1 Melt the butter in a saucepan over a moderate heat.
2 Add the rice and fry, stirring constantly, for 2–3 minutes.
3 Stir in the salt and boiling water or stock.
4 Allow the mixture to boil vigorously for about 3 minutes,
 then cover, lower the heat and simmer for 15–20 minutes
 or until all the liquid has been absorbed.
5 The grains should be tender and separate.
6 Turn off the heat, cover with a clean tea towel, replace the
 lid and leave to 'rest' for about 15 minutes.
7 Gently fluff up the rice with a long-pronged fork, taking
 care not to break the grains, and serve.

4–6 servings

ROZ AHMAR
Red Rice

This is a popular and highly prized rice pilav that has a
reddish-yellow colour due to the use of saffron. In Iraq
turmeric is often substituted since it is cheaper and easier to
obtain.

Prepare as for Roz, but add ¼–½ teaspoon powdered
saffron to the rice while it is frying.

4–6 servings

ROZ SHAMI
Damascus rice

 350 g (12 oz [2 teacups]) long-grain rice, washed
  thoroughly under cold running water and drained

850 ml (28 fl oz [3½ teacups]) water
1 teaspoon salt

1 Place the rice in a saucepan and add the water and salt.
2 Bring quickly to the boil, then lower the heat and simmer
  until the water has almost evaporated.
3 Cover, remove from the heat and leave it to finish cooking
  in its own heat.
4 Leave to rest for 15 minutes, fluff up gently with a long-
  pronged fork and serve.

4–6 servings

ROZ-OU-HAMOUD
Rice with sauce

This is an Egyptian speciality. Its basis is Hamoud – a
versatile sauce which sometimes appears as a soup and
sometimes as a sauce with rice. It is often served after the
meat course, but the better way is to serve it as an accompaniment to chicken dishes.

Traditionally the sauce is made with the bones, giblets etc
of a chicken. It is possible to use stock cubes, but I don't
really recommend it, however convenient it may be, since the
whole essence of eating traditional food is to adhere wherever possible to the traditional ingredients and methods.
Enough of philosophizing, here is the beloved rice dish of the
Egyptians.

Chicken bones, giblets etc, or 1–2 stock cubes
1 turnip, peeled and cut into small pieces
2 potatoes, peeled and cubed
2 leeks, washed thoroughly and thinly sliced
2 sticks celery, coarsely chopped
2 tablespoons finely chopped parsley
2 cloves garlic

Juice 1 lemon
1 teaspoon salt
½ teaspoon black pepper
Rice – prepare as in the recipe Roz or Roz Shami

1 Put all the ingredients in a large saucepan.
2 Add about 900 ml (1½ pints) water
3 Bring to the boil, lower the heat and simmer for about 1
  hour or until the meat will easily come away from the
  bones and the vegetables are very tender and about to disintegrate. Remove any scum which appears on the surface.
4 Remove from the heat, strip the meat from the bones and
  discard the bones.
5 Return the meat to the sauce.
6 Meanwhile prepare the rice to the recipe of your choice.
7 Serve the sauce and rice separately and then pour some of
  the sauce over each serving of rice.

4 servings

ROZ-BIL-SHAGHRIEH
Rice with vermicelli

'May, like the strains of your mother's shagra, your needs be
rich and unending' – Syrian saying.

This is a popular dish with Muslim people throughout the
Middle East. It is specially prepared on the second night of
the New Year (Leylat al aleid) and, traditionally, it is meant
to symbolize long life, rich harvest, prolonged employment
and fertility. In the old days women made their own
vermicelli and macaroni and, indeed, some still do in the
more remote villages.

Contrary to popular belief Marco Polo had nothing to do
with the introduction of spaghetti etc to the Middle East
since the people of that region, thousands of years prior to
his travels, knew and made extensive use of all dough-based

cereals. Indeed, the word 'arsha' – from which shaghrieh originates – is an old Hittite-Urartian word meaning 'shredded dough' and the Arabs, in the course of their conquests, most probably took this dish from the people of the conquered lands.

    100 g (4 oz) chickpeas, soaked overnight
    50 g (2 oz) ghee or butter
    1 onion, finely chopped
    175 g (6 oz) vermicelli
    350 g (12 oz) rice
    900 ml (1½ pints) water
    1 teaspoon salt
    ½ teaspoon black pepper
    3–4 cloves

1 Rinse the soaked chickpeas, place in a pan half filled with water and bring to the boil.
2 Simmer until the chickpeas are tender, removing any scum which may appear, and then drain.
3 Melt the ghee or butter in a large saucepan and sauté the onion until it is golden brown.
4 Break the vermicelli into smallish pieces, 5–7·5 cm (2–3 in), and fry with the onion until dark brown. Take care not to burn.
5 Add the rice and fry for a few more minutes, stirring frequently.
6 Now add the water, salt, pepper and cloves, stir and bring to the boil.
7 Lower the heat and simmer until the water has been absorbed and the rice is tender.
8 Stir in the chickpeas and steam for a few more minutes.
9 This dish is traditionally served with plain yogourt or with a yogourt and cucumber salad called jajig. However it is also good as an accompaniment to roast meats or kebabs.

6 servings

ROZ-BIL-TAMAR
Rice with almonds and dates

A poor Bedouin found a date (which had been thrown away).
'Where shall I go,' he said, 'to eat it in safety?'

Here is a traditional Arabian dish beloved of all Bedouins
and city dwellers. Dates were, and in most of the Gulf States
and Iraq still are, an integral part of an Arab's diet.

> *Plain rice (roz)*
> 50 g (2 oz) butter
> 350 g (12 oz [2 teacups]) rice, washed thoroughly under
>   cold running water and drained
> 1 teaspoon salt
> 850 ml (28 fl oz [3½ teacups]) water or stock, boiling
> *Garnish*
> 50 g (2 oz) butter
> 50 g (2 oz) blanched almonds
> 75 g (3 oz) stoned dates, chopped
> 50 g (2 oz) raisins or sultanas
> 1 teaspoon rosewater

1 Cook the rice, following the instructions for plain rice –
   roz – see page 181.
2 While the rice is 'resting' melt half the butter in a large
   frying pan.
3 Now add the almonds and fry them, stirring frequently
   until they begin to turn light golden. Do not overcook at
   this stage.
4 Add the remaining butter, dates, raisins or sultanas and
   fry for a few more minutes, stirring very frequently.
5 Remove from the heat and stir in the rosewater.
6 To serve, spoon the rice into a serving bowl and arrange
   the fruit and nut mixture over the top.

4 servings

KITRY
Rice and lentil pilav

This recipe from Iraq is popular throughout the Gulf States and Kuwait. Its origin is undoubtedly India and kitry is, in fact, an Arabized version of the classic Indian khichri – a rice and lentil dish. The English kedgeree is another version of the simple Indian recipe. Kitry is often eaten on its own, but is at its best when accompanying cooked vegetables or a roast meat or chicken dish.

100 g (4 oz) whole brown lentils
2 tablespoons oil
2 cloves garlic, finely chopped
1 tablespoon tomato purée
½ teaspoon turmeric
½ teaspoon salt
250 g (9 oz [1½ teacups]) long-grain rice, washed
600 ml (1 pint [2½ teacups]) water or stock

1 Place the lentils in a saucepan with sufficient water to cover by about 5 cm (2 in) and simmer until the lentils are just tender.
2 Strain the lentils into a colander and set aside.
3 Heat the oil in a large saucepan and sauté the garlic, stirring occasionally for 2 minutes.
4 Add the tomato purée, turmeric and salt. Fry, stirring frequently, for a further 2 minutes.
5 Add the rice and lentils and toss in the mixture until well coated.
6 Pour in the water or stock, bring to the boil, reduce the heat, cover and simmer until the moisture has been absorbed and the rice and lentils are tender.
7 Leave to rest for 10–15 minutes and serve.

4 servings

ROZ-BIL-BETINGAN
Rice and aubergine pilav

This is a dish from Saudi Arabia or, to be more precise, from the Holy City of Mecca – where T. E. Lawrence found in his *Seven Pillars of Wisdom* that the mass of citizens were foreigners, Egyptians, Indians, Javanese, Africans and others. It is not therefore surprising to find this rich rice pilav that is nearer to the Indian cuisine than to the Arab one in the heart of Arabia with its final touch of 'flaked coconut'. No doubt the spice routes, as much as Muhammed, had a lot to do with the evolution of this recipe. It has a delicate aroma and flavour and is excellent with plain or boiled meat.

    ¼ teaspoon mustard seeds
    ½ teaspoon poppy seeds
    2 whole cloves
    ¼ teaspoon turmeric
    ¼ teaspoon ground cumin
    ½ teaspoon ground cinnamon
    ½ teaspoon cayenne pepper
    ¼ teaspoon black pepper
    1 tablespoon peanuts
    6 tablespoons butter
    1 aubergine
    1 onion, finely chopped
    350 g (12 oz [2 teacups]) cooked rice – see recipe for Roz
        Shami, page 182
    25 g (1 oz) flaked coconut

1 Put the mustard seeds, poppy seeds, cloves, turmeric, cumin, cinnamon, cayenne and black pepper and peanuts in a mortar and pestle and pound until everything is ground to a powder and well mixed.
2 Melt 2 tablespoons of the butter in a saucepan, add the mixed spices, stir and cook for 2 minutes.

3 Wash and dry the aubergine, slice off the head and tail and then cut into 5 mm (¼ in) cubes.

4 Add the aubergine to the spice mixture and toss until well coated.

5 Cook very gently, stirring frequently, until the aubergine is soft and tender.

6 Melt 2 more tablespoons of butter in a large saucepan, add the onion and fry until it is soft and lightly browned.

7 Add the remaining 2 tablespoons of butter and leave it to melt.

8 Add the rice and fry, stirring all the time, for about 5 minutes or until the rice is heated through.

9 Stir the aubergine mixture into the rice and cook for a further minute or two.

10 Arrange the rice mixture on a large plate, garnish with the flaked coconut and serve immediately.

6 servings

MUJADDARAH
Rice and lentils

This is a traditional dish sometimes called 'Esau's favourite', and it is mentioned by the medieval writer al-Baghdadi. In the old days meat was also included, but not so today. It is a very popular substantial dish that is often eaten on its own, although a tossed salad and/or pickles and olives are excellent accompaniments. A bowl of yogourt will enhance it even further.

Mujaddarah is popular throughout the Arab world, but especially with the Syrian and Lebanese peasant folk. It is also highly prized by the Armenians who, however, replace the rice with burghul (cracked wheat).

I come from a family of Mujaddarah lovers. My father, brother and cousins swear by it and although I, personally, have never been enamoured of this dish I must confess that, every now and then, I have a real penchant for a dish of burghul mujaddarah topped with dark, crisp fried onions.

175 g (6 oz) whole brown lentils, washed and drained
900 ml (1½ pints) cold water
200 ml (⅓ pint) olive or cooking oil
2 large onions, thinly sliced
2 teaspoons salt
½ teaspoon black pepper
300 ml (½ pint) boiling water
175 g (6 oz) rice, washed

1 Put the lentils in a large saucepan, cover with the cold water and bring to the boil.
2 Lower the heat, cover and cook for 25–30 minutes or until the lentils are almost cooked and the water mostly evaporated.
3 Meanwhile, in a frying pan, heat the oil, add the sliced onions and fry, stirring frequently, until they are dark golden, but take care not to burn.
4 Reserve half of the onion and the oil; stir the other half into the lentils.
5 Add the salt, pepper and boiling water and bring to the boil.
6 Stir in the rice and bring to the boil again.
7 Lower the heat, cover and simmer for 15–20 minutes or until the lentils and rice are tender and the water absorbed.
8 Remove from the heat and leave to stand for 10–15 minutes.
9 Pile the mujaddarah on to a plate and garnish with the remaining onions and oil.

4–6 servings

Cooked Vegetables

MSHAT ARNABEET	*Cauliflower cheese*
BADENJAN WYA CHOBAN	*Aubergine casserole*
PATATAS MUSULIYEH	*Potatoes with yogourt*
FASOLYEH-BI-BANADOORA	*Beans with tomatoes*
BASAL-BI-SABANEGH	*Spinach and onions*
TIFFAH-BIL-FUREN	*Apples stuffed with rice and raisins*
TARTOUFA-BI-BANADOORA	*Artichokes with tomatoes*
BAMIA BASRANI	*Okra with tomatoes*

MSHAT ARNABEET
Cauliflower cheese

A simple recipe from Jordan which is cheap and easy to prepare and makes an excellent accompaniment to all meat dishes. Nutmeg gives the dish its own particular fragrant and soothing flavour.

1 cauliflower
225 g (½ lb) grated cheese (Cheddar is very suitable)
2 tablespoons flour
1 egg
150 ml (¼ pint) milk
1 teaspoon salt
½ teaspoon black pepper
½ teaspoon nutmeg
Oil for frying
Garnish
2 tablespoons finely grated parsley
1 lemon, cut into wedges

1 Wash the cauliflower, break into florets and dry with kitchen paper.
2 In a large bowl mix the cheese, flour, egg and milk together to form a thick batter.
3 Season with the salt, pepper and nutmeg.
4 Heat some oil in a large frying pan.
5 Now dip the florets, one at a time, into the cheese batter and then fry gently until they are soft and golden.
6 Arrange the cauliflower cheese on a large plate, sprinkle with the parsley and garnish with the lemon wedges.

4 servings

BADENJAN WYA CHOBAN
Aubergine casserole

A beautiful dish from Syria, with Ottoman overtones. It is
also popular in southern Turkey and is known as Shepherd's
Casserole. It is a filling dish and can be eaten as a main meal
with an accompanying side salad. However, I like it as a
vegetable dish accompanying roast meat or kebabs.

150 ml (¼ pint) cooking oil
2 eggs
1 tablespoon milk
225 g (½ lb) kashkaval or kefalotyri cheese, finely grated
    (if unobtainable use Cheddar)
½ teaspoon salt
¼ teaspoon black pepper
2 medium aubergines cut crossways into 3 mm (¼ in) slices
About 6 large tomatoes, sliced
4 tablespoons finely chopped parsley
Sauce
1 egg
1 onion, finely chopped
1 teaspoon chopped chives
½ teaspoon sweet marjoram
½ teaspoon salt
¼ teaspoon black pepper
2 tablespoons tomato purée
Few tablespoons water

1 Heat the oil in a large frying pan.
2 Mix together in a bowl the eggs, milk, 2 tablespoons of
   the grated cheese and the salt and pepper.
3 Dip each aubergine slice into the egg mixture and then
   fry, turning once, until soft and golden brown.
4 Remove each slice and drain on kitchen paper until they
   are all fried.

5 Arrange half the aubergine slices over the base of a lightly buttered casserole dish.

6 Cover with a layer of sliced tomatoes.

7 Sprinkle half the grated cheese and chopped parsley over the tomatoes.

8 Repeat this process with the remaining aubergine and tomato slices, cheese and parsley.

9 Put all the ingredients for the sauce into a bowl and mix well until blended.

10 Pour this evenly over the surface of the casserole.

11 Cook in an oven preheated to 180°C (350°F, Gas Mark 4) for about 45 minutes or until the vegetables are well cooked.

12 Remove from the oven and leave to cool for 5 minutes.

13 Serve by cutting it into wedges or squares.

6 servings

PATATAS MUSULIYEH
Potatoes with yogourt

A Kurdish dish from Iraq, this recipe has a greater affinity to the cuisines of Armenia and Iran than to that of the Arabs. This is not surprising as the Kurds are a Muslim people of Aryan origin and are thus ethnically nearer to the Iranians than the Arabians. It goes well with all meat dishes.

6 large potatoes, peeled
25 g (1 oz) butter or ghee
3 tablespoons yogourt
4 egg yolks
½ teaspoon sweet marjoram
½ teaspoon cayenne pepper
1 teaspoon salt
2 tablespoons sesame seeds
4 tablespoons very finely chopped walnuts

3 tablespoons toasted breadcrumbs
Oil for frying
Garnish
Lettuce leaves
Tarragon leaves
Spring onions and radishes

1 Cook the potatoes in boiling, salted water until they are
   tender.
2 Drain the potatoes and mash them until smooth.
3 Put the mashed potatoes into a large bowl with the butter
   and yogourt and stir until well blended.
4 Now add 2 of the egg yolks and the marjoram, pepper,
   salt and sesame seeds and mix well.
5 Take a spoonful of the potato mixture and roll it between
   wet palms to form a walnut-sized ball. Repeat the process
   with the rest of the mixture.
6 Beat the remaining egg yolks in a small bowl.
7 Mix the walnuts and breadcrumbs together on a plate.
8 Meanwhile heat the oil in a large frying pan.
9 Dip each potato ball into the beaten egg and then roll it in
   the walnut mix.
10 Fry a few at a time, turning until they are golden all over.
   This will take only a few minutes. Do not overcook.
11 Drain on kitchen paper and then arrange on a bed of
   lettuce leaves.
12 Garnish with the tarragon, spring onions, radishes and/
   or any other available herbs.

6 servings

FASOLYEH-BI-BANADOORA
Beans with tomatoes

A typical Middle Eastern vegetable dish popular throughout
the region, a family favourite. The same method of prepara-

tion can be applied to other vegetables such as broad beans,
peas, carrots etc. This dish has an added advantage in that it
is just as delicious served hot, warm or cold.

> 450 g (1 lb) green beans
> 1 large onion, finely chopped
> About 90 ml (3 fl oz) olive or vegetable oil
> 1 teaspoon salt
> ½ teaspoon black pepper
> ½ teaspoon allspice
> 2 large tomatoes, coarsely chopped
> 450 ml (¾ pint) water

1 Wash the beans, snip off the ends and cut into 5 cm (2 in)
  pieces.
2 Heat the oil in a large saucepan and sauté the onion until
  soft but not brown.
3 Add the beans, salt, pepper and allspice.
4 Cover and cook for 5 minutes.
5 Uncover, add the tomatoes and water and cook over a
  medium heat for about 30 minutes, stirring occasionally,
  until the beans are tender.
6 Serve warm.

6 servings

BASAL-BI-SABANEGH
Spinach and onions

'If an onion causes his loved one rejoicings, what then shall
we say to sugar?' (Said of people who bestow admiration
upon trifling objects.)

This is a recipe from Tripoli – famed for its kibbeh dishes,
melons, ancient port and the above dish. For centuries
Tripoli, with Acre and Antioch, was a centre of international
commerce and vied, with its wealth, with such prosperous

places as Egypt, Constantinople, Baghdad and the Crusader cities of Europe. There is a great deal of the Crusades still in evidence around Tripoli, not least in the physical appearance of the people who take pride in their 'European' looks.

450 g (1 lb) fresh spinach
75 ml (2½ fl oz) oil
2 onions, thinly sliced
Juice 1 lemon
1 clove garlic, finely chopped
½ teaspoon salt
¼ teaspoon black pepper
¼ teaspoon dill

1 Wash the spinach thoroughly several times in cold water and then pat dry with kitchen paper.
2 Half fill a large saucepan with lightly salted water, bring to the boil, add the spinach and cook for 5–7 minutes.
3 Strain into a colander and when cool enough to handle squeeze out the excess moisture from the spinach.
4 Coarsely chop the leaves and arrange them on a large serving plate.
5 Meanwhile heat the oil in a frying pan and sauté the onions until they are soft and golden brown.
6 Remove half the onions from the pan and set aside.
7 To the onions left in the pan add the lemon juice, garlic, salt, pepper and dill.
8 Mix these well together and spoon over the spinach.
9 Just before serving garnish with the remaining fried onions.
10 Serve cold with cold meats or poultry.

4 servings

TIFFAH-BIL-FUREN
Apples stuffed with rice and raisins

'A house from which thou eatest, do not pray for its destruction' – Egyptian saying.

This rather sophisticated vegetable recipe is highly prized in Iraq and is very similar to certain Iranian dishes, eg the classic Dolma Sib (stuffed apples). I have seen this dish sometimes served as a sweet, but I believe it is far more successful as an accompanying vegetable. Make sure the apples are of a good size and are a cooking variety.

    4 large cooking apples
    4 teaspoons sugar
    75 g (3 oz) cooked rice
    2 tablespoons raisins
    2 teaspoons pine kernels or chopped walnuts or almonds
    2 tablespoons melted butter
    1 teaspoon cinnamon
    Hot water

1 Wash and dry the apples.
2 Cut a 1 cm (½ in) slice off the top of each apple and keep to one side for later use.
3 With an apple corer remove each core and some of the flesh leaving a shell about 5 mm (¼ in) thick. Take care not to damage the shell.
4 Arrange the apples side by side in an ovenproof dish.
5 Sprinkle 1 teaspoon of the sugar into each apple.
6 In a small bowl mix together the rice, raisins, nuts and melted butter.
7 Fill each apple carefully with this mixture. Do not pack too tightly as the rice and especially the raisins will expand during cooking.
8 Sprinkle a little of the cinnamon on to each apple.
9 Now cover the apples with their tops.

10 Add sufficient hot water to come a little more than halfway up the apples.
11 Cook in an oven preheated to 180°C (350°F, Gas Mark 4)
for 30–40 minutes, or until the apples are soft, but firm.
The time will depend a bit on the type and quality of the
apples.
12 Serve as a vegetable dish accompanying any roast meat
or poultry.

4 servings

TARTOUFA-BI-BANADOORA
Artichokes with tomatoes

'Wallah – by God – the man is as difficult to unravel as a
tartoufa' – Arab saying.

Tartoufa is the Arabic name for Jerusalem artichokes, an
extremely popular vegetable in the East, with its characteristic knobbly texture that makes it rather difficult to peel –
hence the above saying. Artichokes are found in Britain and
the USA although they can be rather expensive and are not
always available. This is an exquisite-tasting side dish which
can also be eaten as a mezzeh.

900 g (2 lb) Jerusalem artichokes
4–5 tablespoons olive oil
1 onion, finely chopped
2 cloves garlic, halved
3 tomatoes, blanched, peeled and chopped
1 tablespoon tomato purée
½ teaspoon salt
½ teaspoon dill
¼ teaspoon black pepper
Juice of 1 small lemon
2 tablespoons finely chopped parsley

1 Wash the artichokes and then peel and wash again.
2 Heat the olive oil in a large saucepan and sauté the onion and garlic until golden brown.
3 Now add the artichokes and roll in the oil until they are covered.
4 Add the tomatoes and, with a wooden spoon, squash them into the oil and onion mixture.
5 Add the tomato purée, salt, dill and pepper and half the lemon juice and stir thoroughly.
6 Cover the vegetables with water and leave to simmer for 30–45 minutes or until the artichokes are tender and the sauce is thick.
7 Serve as a side dish to roast meats.
8 Garnish just before serving with more lemon juice if you wish and with the parsley sprinkled over the top.

6 servings

BAMIA BASRANI
Okra with tomatoes

This is an Iraqi recipe which makes use of turmeric, coriander and garlic. Okra – ladies' fingers – is one of the basic vegetables of Iraq where the peasants make soups, salads and wholesome dishes from this oft-neglected vegetable. Indeed, often the word 'bamia' is used in a derogatory way when describing someone who is rather sullen, stupid or ignorant.

Do not purchase the long, fat okra that is often found in Indian stores as they will easily disintegrate when cooked and they contain many large seeds. Buy the smallest you can find. You can buy tinned okra from many stores, but if you use these then take care as they need little cooking. This dish, as with most olive-oil-based dishes, can be eaten hot or cold, but I prefer the warm version. It makes a fine accompaniment to meat or poultry dishes.

675 g (1½ lb) fresh okra or one 750–850 g (28–30 oz) tin
  okra
5 tablespoons olive oil
2 onions, thinly sliced
2 cloves garlic, quartered
450 g (1 lb) tomatoes, blanched, peeled and sliced
½ teaspoon turmeric
½ teaspoon coriander
½ teaspoon salt
¼ teaspoon black pepper
Juice 1 lemon

1 Wash the okra thoroughly and cut off the stems taking
  care not to cut into the vegetable.
2 Heat the oil in a large saucepan and sauté the onions and
  garlic until soft and lightly browned.
3 Add the okra and cook for a few minutes, stirring gently
  but frequently.
4 Now add the tomatoes and continue frying for a few more
  minutes.
5 Add the turmeric, coriander, salt and pepper.
6 Cover with water, bring quickly to the boil then lower the
  heat and simmer from 45–60 minutes or until the okra is
  tender.
7 Stir in the lemon juice and cook for a further 10–15
  minutes. If using the tinned okra then the cooking time
  will be much less – just enough to make the okra tender
  but not mushy.
8 Serve hot or cold.

6 servings

Sauces

TARATOR	*Pine-nuts and olive oil sauce*
TARATOR FENDUKH	*Bread and hazelnut sauce*
HILLBEH	*Fenugreek and tomato sauce*
SALSA-TEL-LOZ	*Almond sauce*
BEID-BI-LAMOUN	*Egg and lemon sauce*
SALSA	*Herbs and vinegar sauce*
SALSA-TEL-SAMAK	*Milk and shrimp sauce*
MARET LABEN MA KIRFAH	*Cinnamon and yogourt sauce*

TARATOR
Pine-nuts and olive oil sauce

There are several tarator sauces throughout the Middle East. They are probably of a pre-Arab period and originate from the Levant, ie the Mediterranean coastline stretching from southern Turkey through Syria, Lebanon and modern Israel.

Some tarator sauces have a basis of tahina (seasame paste). These, eg Tahiniyeh, are normally eaten as dips. Others are lighter in consistency, eg Tarator-bi-Tahina, and are used as sauces over fish dishes.

This Syrian recipe omits tahina, but makes use of olive oil and pine-nuts. It is a delicious sauce and can be used with fish, cold meats and all kinds of poultry. As pine-nuts are very expensive and difficult to find you can use almonds instead, although the results are not quite so authentic.

    100 g (4 oz) pine-nuts or almonds
    1 teaspoon salt
    2 cloves garlic, crushed
    Olive oil
    Juice of 1 lemon – or more, depending on taste

1 Pound the nuts using a mortar and pestle, or grind in a blender.
2 Add the salt and crushed garlic to the nuts and continue to blend until well mixed together.
3 Scrape the mixture into a bowl, add about 4–6 tablespoons of olive oil and mix thoroughly.

4 Add the lemon juice and stir well. The sauce should be of a thick, smooth consistency but if it is too thick add a little water, but do not over-dilute.
5 Taste and adjust seasoning if necessary.
6 Pour into a bowl and serve with fish, chicken or cold meats.

4–6 servings

TARATOR FENDUKH
Bread and hazelnut sauce

A speciality of Iraq, this is based on the principle of the tarator sauces, but not made with tahina. Instead it makes use of hazelnuts – northern Iraq producing the finest quality in the Middle East – and crustless bread. This simple sauce has that earthy flavour of hazelnuts and goes extremely well with meat and chicken dishes.

  1 thick slice of bread, crusts removed
  225 g (½ lb) roasted hazelnuts
  1–2 cloves garlic, crushed
  Juice of 1 lemon
  1 teaspoon salt
  1 teaspoon paprika
  A little chicken stock or water
  Garnish
  1 tablespoon chopped parsley
  ½ teaspoon paprika

1 Soak the bread in water and then squeeze it dry.
2 Put the bread in a liquidizer together with the nuts, garlic and salt and blend for a minute or two.
3 Add the lemon juice, paprika and 3–4 tablespoons of either chicken stock or water and blend for a little longer.
4 By now the sauce should have the thickness of double

cream. If not, then add a little more liquid but do not over-dilute.
5 Pour the sauce into a tureen and garnish with the parsley and paprika.

6 servings

HILLBEH
Fenugreek and tomato sauce

This recipe is from Yemen.

> 2 tablespoons fenugreek seeds, or 1 tablespoon fenugreek powder
> 200 ml (⅓ pint) water
> 3 tomatoes, blanched, peeled and chopped
> 3 cloves garlic, finely chopped
> ½ teaspoon salt
> ½ teaspoon caraway seeds
> ½ teaspoon coriander seeds, or ¼ teaspoon ground coriander
> ½ teaspoon cayenne pepper, or more if you like hot dishes
> 1½ teaspoon ground cumin
> Pinch ground cardamon

1 If using fenugreek seeds, crush them to a fine powder in a mortar and pestle.
2 Put the powder in a small bowl, add the water and leave for 3 hours.
3 Sieve the tomatoes into a large bowl, pushing through as much pulp as possible.
4 Stir in the fenugreek mixture.
5 In another bowl mix thoroughly all the remaining ingredients and mash them to a smooth mixture.
6 Add this to the tomato mixture and stir vigorously for a few minutes.

7 Serve as a relish with roast meats.

4–6 servings

SALSA-TEL-LOZ
Almond sauce

This recipe is also known as Salsa Shami – Damascus sauce, since it is a favourite of that region. It is a beautifully delicate sauce that is beloved of all Syrians, and is to them what Hamoud sauce is to the Egyptians. It is a must with the simple Roz Shami and most other rice pilavs, and it also often accompanies chicken dishes.

    50 g (2 oz) ground almonds
    600 ml (1 pint) chicken stock
    1 clove garlic, crushed
    1 teaspoon honey, or sugar
    Juice of 1 lemon
    1 tablespoon parsley, finely chopped
    ½ teaspoon salt
    Pinch white pepper
    Garnish
    1 tablespoon finely chopped parsley
    1 tablespoon pine kernels or pistachio nuts, coarsely
      chopped

1 Mix the almonds and chicken stock together in a saucepan and bring slowly to the boil, stirring frequently.
2 Add the garlic, salt, white pepper, honey or sugar, parsley and lemon juice.
3 Lower the heat and simmer for 20–30 minutes, stirring frequently. The mixture should now resemble a thick sauce.
4 Pour the sauce into a tureen and garnish with the parsley and chopped nuts.

4–6 servings

BEID-BI-LAMOUN
Egg and lemon sauce

This popular sauce appears everywhere from Greece to the northern Gulf States. It is very popular with the Turks and the Armenians, but I suspect that for its origin we must look to Greece or to Byzantium. Beid-bi-lamoun is the Greek avgolemono and it is unquestionably the national sauce of that land. The Arab people, especially the Syrians, Lebanese and Egyptians, also make great use of this delightful sauce – a vestige perhaps of the centuries of Greek and Ottoman rule. As I have often maintained – rulers may come and go, the names of nations may change, but the food and music remain – Beid-bi-Lamoun, Avgolemono, Terbiyeli etc have survived the passage of time simply because they are good.

Traditionally this sauce accompanies fish dishes, hot or cold. However the recipe here is for chicken dishes and it can also accompany rice pilavs. If you wish to adapt it for a fish dish, merely use fish stock instead of chicken stock.

450–600 ml (¾–1 pint) chicken stock (use fish stock if preparing a fish dish)
½ teaspoon salt
¼ teaspoon black pepper
1 tablespoon cornflour
3 egg yolks
Juice of 2 small lemons

1 Pour the stock into a saucepan and season with the salt and pepper.
2 Beat the egg yolks in a small bowl and then add the lemon juice, stirring constantly.
3 Pour the egg mixture slowly into the stock and stir well.
4 Mix the cornflour with a little water and add to the pan.
5 Heat the sauce gently, stirring constantly using a wooden spoon, for about 20 minutes. Do not bring it to the boil or

it will curdle. The sauce should, by now, have a smooth, paste-like consistency.
6 Serve hot or cold.

6 servings

SALSA
Herbs and vinegar sauce

'Not a grain of mustard seed falls from his hands' – Proverb.

A family favourite popular in Syria and Lebanon, there are as many versions of this charming recipe as there are good cooks. There are no set rules as to the types of herbs used and often the final choice will depend on what is available and on personal taste.

This sauce is really only successful when made with fresh herbs. The ingredients given below are those used by my mother, handed down to her, no doubt, by her mother etc.

Salsa is excellent with fish, poultry and all cuts of cold meat.

6 tablespoons olive oil
½ teaspoon salt
¼ teaspoon dry mustard
¼ teaspoon cayenne pepper
4 tablespoons vinegar
½ teaspoon tarragon, finely chopped
1 teaspoon parsley, finely chopped
½ teaspoon basil, finely chopped
½ teaspoon oregano, finely chopped
Pinch cumin

1 In a bowl mix together the oil, salt, mustard, pepper and vinegar.
2 Add all the remaining ingredients and stir well.
3 Set aside for about ½ hour.

4 Just before serving, strain the sauce through a fine sieve or piece of muslin.
5 Spoon the sauce over fish, chicken or pieces of cold meat.

4–6 servings

SALSA-TEL-SAMAK
Milk and shrimp sauce

This is an interesting recipe from Palestine, very popular with the sophisticated Levantines who spend a great deal of their leisure time discussing politics, with great passion, and eating a lot of pilav, accompanied by the sauce in our recipe – at least I like to think so. However, although I am sure Middle Eastern people do heatedly and passionately discuss politics and eat well, they do not all accompany their pilavs with this sauce since I know for a fact that this recipe, given to me by one of my uncles in Beirut – a hotelier family of three generations – smacks too much of European haute cuisine.

Salsa-tel-Samak is Arabic, I am sure of that, but as to how many of the original ingredients have remained in this recipe, I am not certain. It is still a fine delicate sauce which when served with a rice pilav of your choice can be a meal in itself. It is also excellent with fish kebabs.

600 ml (1 pint) milk
½ teaspoon salt
½ teaspoon black pepper
1 tablespoon cornflour
4 tablespoons grated feta or Cheddar cheese
275 g (10 oz) button mushrooms
275 g (10 oz) shrimps (use tinned or frozen ones if you cannot get hold of fresh ones)
Garnish
1 tablespoon finely chopped parsley

1 Place the milk in a saucepan and bring to the boil.
2 Season with the salt and pepper.
3 Blend the cornflour with 2 tablespoons of the hot milk.
4 Pour the remainder of the hot milk into the cornflour and stir until well blended.
5 Return the mixture to the saucepan and heat, stirring constantly, until the sauce thickens.
6 Remove the pan from the heat and add the cheese.
7 Stir until the cheese has melted.
8 Add the mushrooms and shrimps. Simmer, stirring frequently, over a very low heat for about 5 minutes, until the mushrooms and shrimps are just cooked.
9 Sprinkle with the parsley and serve.

4–6 servings

MARET LABEN MA KIRFAH
Cinnamon and yogourt sauce

This yogourt sauce is traditionally served with roast meats as well as with salads and vegetables.

300 ml (½ pint) yogourt
2 teaspoons sugar
Garnish
1 teaspoon ground cinnamon

1 Pour the yogourt into a serving bowl.
2 Add the sugar and mix well.
3 Sprinkle with the cinnamon and serve.

Savouries, Bread and Yogourt

KAAHK	*Savoury cakes*
KAAHK-BI-TEMAR	*Date cakes*
KAAHK RAMAZAN	*Festive cakes*
KHUBZ ARABI	*Arab bread*
MANNAEESH	*Thyme bread*
KHUBZ BASALI	*Onion bread*
KHUBZ SAJ	*Thin bread*
KHUBZ TABOUN	*Mosaic bread*
LABAN	*Yogourt*

PALM TREE

They seek the great store of water below with their roots
so that they drink of it plenty till they are satisfied.
They vie in tallness with the two precipitous sides of Ushann
which face them; they bear abundantly and care
Not at all for years of drought.
Their topmost heads of foliage waving in every wind are
Like girls that pull at one another's hair . . .
The guest travels, then halts under them in a halting place
Of honour, until the time comes for him to go his way.
This then, is our wealth and the reward of it remains to us!

                    al-Massar-al Tamin, seventh century AD

KAAHK
Savoury cakes

'My mother writes of the brightest moonlight she has ever seen
in her life "which makes everything look like snow," and of the
azure blue sky through a trellis of vine-leaves. The milkman shouting halib! halib! in a queer sort of wail, mispronouncing every bit as
badly as a London milkman . . .

   As soon as the sun is up a flock of goats comes and waits to be
milked. People come out in pink dressing-gowns with jugs to be
filled. There are also cows, each with a calf attached by a string . . .
Then, at an extraordinarily early hour, men came past carrying
trays of "khakis" on their heads, like muffin men (a khaki is a large
ring or hoop of bread covered with sesame seed).'

        In Aleppo Once, T. Altounyan, J. Murray, 1965, London

You will find similar cakes in most Cypriot bakeries and
shops. They are excellent for 'dunking' – a rather nasty habit

of mine! Below is a typical recipe although it does vary a little
from region to region and family to family.

　　450 g (1 lb) plain flour
　　1 teaspoon salt
　　15 g (½ oz) fresh yeast, or 8 g (¼ oz) dried yeast
　　300 ml (½ pint) tepid water
　　Pinch sugar
　　100 g (4 oz) unsalted butter or margarine
　　½ teaspoon cumin
　　½ teaspoon coriander
　　1 egg, beaten
　　Sesame seeds

1　Sift the flour and salt into a bowl.
2　Dissolve the yeast in a little water, add the sugar and let it
　　rest for 10–15 minutes until it begins to froth.
3　Melt the butter or margarine and leave it to cool.
4　Mix the cumin and coriander into the flour and then
　　make a well in the centre.
5　Add the butter and yeast mixture and knead.
6　Add the water, a little at a time, and knead until the
　　dough is firm, but not hard. Add more water if necessary
　　and knead for 10–15 minutes until the mixture is smooth
　　and comes away from the bowl and the hands easily.
7　Cover the bowl with a damp cloth and let the dough rest
　　for about 2 hours until it has doubled in size.
8　Flour a board, take walnut-sized lumps of dough and roll
　　into thin strips about 15 × 10 cm (6 × 4 in).
9　Roll each one into a cigarette shape, form into a circle
　　and press the two ends firmly together.
10　Arrange the cakes on greased baking sheets leaving
　　about 2·5 cm (1 in) between each and then brush with the
　　beaten egg and sprinkle with sesame seeds.

11 Bake in an oven preheated to 180°C (350°F, Gas Mark 4) for 25–30 minutes until crisp and golden brown.

About 25–30 cakes

KAAHK-BI-TEMAR
Date cakes

Kaahks are savoury cakes, biscuits, cookies or whatever name you care to give. There are many versions, some with nuts or fruit, some plain or some with dates as in this recipe. They are normally made in large quantities and stored to last several weeks. Served with tea or coffee, they are perfect eaten by themselves or with jam or cheese.

I am not sure whether the concept of 'dry bread' is Greek, Ancient Egyptian or Cappadocian. I suspect the latter since there are more kaahk-type savouries in southern Turkey and northern Syria than anywhere else in the Middle East.

450 g (1 lb) plain flour
$\frac{1}{2}$ teaspoon salt
300 ml ($\frac{1}{2}$ pint) tepid water
450 g (1 lb) dates
1 level teaspoon ground nutmeg
Icing sugar

1 Sift the flour and salt into a large bowl.
2 Make a well in the centre, add the water and knead to make a firm, but not hard, dough.
3 Lightly flour a working surface and continue kneading the dough for about 5 minutes.
4 Return the dough to the bowl, cover and leave for 30 minutes.
5 Meanwhile stone the dates and pound the fruit to a pulp in a mortar.
6 Add the nutmeg, mix thoroughly and set aside.

7 Uncover the dough, punch it down and knead for a few more minutes.

8 Divide the dough into 4 portions.

9 Lightly flour a board and roll out each portion until it is 3 mm (⅛ in) thick.

10 Cut the dough into strips approximately 15 cm (6 in) long and 5 cm (2 in) wide.

11 Take 1 teaspoon of the date mixture, form it into a cigarette/sausage shape and place it along one of the long sides of the dough strips, 2·5 cm (1 in) from one edge.

12 Roll the pastry over the date mixture and then over the remaining dough strip to form a cigarette shape and pinch the ends together to seal them. (The whole procedure is very similar to making a roll-up cigarette.)

13 Continue the process until all the dough and date mixture has been used.

14 Grease 2 or 3 baking sheets, arrange the kaahks leaving about 2·5 cm (1 in) between them and bake in an oven pre-heated to 180°C (350°F, Gas Mark 4) for 30–40 minutes until golden brown.

15 Allow the kaahks to cool and then dust with sieved icing sugar.

About 35–40 biscuits

KAAHK RAMAZAN
Festive cakes

'The corn passes from hand to hand, but comes at last to the mill' – Egyptian saying.

The crescent moon became a symbol of the Ottoman Empire about 1589 and thus symbolized the Muhammedan religion. Kaahk Ramazan or Khubz Ramazan are rolls made from puff pastry or buttered doughs and generally baked in a crescent shape, although there are a few other fairly popular shapes, eg round and star.

Interestingly enough it is reputed that the now famed French croissants originated in 1686 in Budapest where the Turks were defeated and the bakers were rewarded with the privilege of making pastries in the form of a crescent – the symbol of the Ottoman Empire. This is a good story, but not entirely true. The truth is much simpler since the crescent shape was also the symbol of a much older religion – that of the Goddess Diana, or Anahita of the Persians, and the crescent-shaped breads were very popular in Middle Eastern lands much before Budapest was even planned.

Kaahk Ramazan are traditionally only baked during the holy festive period of Ramadan when, from sunrise to sunset, all good Muslims do not allow even a drop of water to pass through their lips. Towards evening fresh kaahks, in different shapes, are purchased and then heartily consumed. For the lunar month of Ramazan my grandfather's bakeries literally churned out thousands upon thousands of full moon, star and crescent-shaped kaahks and quite a few of them were consumed by non-Muslims such as I who adored the soft, flaky and slightly aromatic flavour of a Kaahk Ramazan.

Below is a simplified recipe for these cakes. I have used cinnamon, but I know some people like vanilla essence or rosewater.

15 g (½ oz) fresh yeast, or 8 g (¼ oz) dried yeast
250 ml (8 fl oz) tepid milk
3 tablespoons sugar
450 g (1 lb) plain flour
1 teaspoon salt
½ teaspoon ground cinnamon, or 1 teaspoon of vanilla
    essence or rosewater
150 g (5 oz) unsalted butter

3 eggs, lightly beaten
1 tablespoon poppy seeds
1 tablespoon sesame seeds

1 In a small bowl dissolve the yeast in 3–4 tablespoons of the milk.
2 Add 1 tablespoon of the sugar, mix well and leave to rest for about 15 minutes or until frothy.
3 Into a large warmed bowl sift the flour, salt and cinnamon (if using) and stir in the remaining sugar.
4 Add 25 g (1 oz) of the butter cut into small pieces and rub it into the flour until the mixture resembles fine breadcrumbs.
5 Make a well in the centre of the flour and add the yeast mixture, the rest of the milk, two-thirds of the beaten egg mixture and the vanilla or rosewater (if using).
6 Using the fingers, mix for 10–15 minutes until you have a soft, smooth dough.
7 Cover the bowl with a damp cloth and refrigerate for 1 hour.
8 Place the remaining butter between two pieces of greaseproof paper and using a rolling pin, roll out the butter into a rectangle 15 × 10 cm (6 × 4 in).
9 Place the flattened butter in the refrigerator.
10 Remove the dough from the refrigerator and knead for a further 5 minutes.
11 Lightly flour a working surface and roll out the dough into an oblong measuring about 30 × 20 cm (12 × 8 in).
12 Remove the butter from the refrigerator, unwrap and place in the centre of the dough.
13 Carefully fold over all four edges to completely enclose the butter.
14 Roll out into a strip 30–38 cm (12–15 in) long and then fold the bottom third up to the centre and the top third

down to the centre.

15 Wrap in greaseproof and return to the refrigerator for a further 15 minutes.

16 Repeat steps 14 and 15 twice more. After the second rolling refrigerate for 1 hour.

17 Roll out the dough into a rectangle measuring about 60 × 40 cm (24 × 16 in) and about 5 mm ($\frac{1}{4}$ in) thick.

18 Cut the dough down the middle and then cut each half into three 20 cm (8 in) squares.

19 Now cut each square in half diagonally to form triangles.

20 Roll each triangle up quite tightly from the broadest end to the tip and then pull into a crescent shape and join the ends together.

21 Place the cake on ungreased baking sheets with the tips underneath, cover with a damp cloth and leave for 20–30 minutes until they have doubled in size.

22 Preheat the oven to 220°C (425°F, Gas Mark 7).

23 Separate the joined ends of each kaahk and then brush all the kaahks with the remaining beaten egg.

24 Sprinkle half with the sesame seeds and half with the poppy seeds.

25 Bake for about 10 minutes until golden brown and then remove from the oven, allow to cool and serve fresh.

About 20–25 cakes

KHUBZ ARABI
Arab bread

'On my family's bread I swear I tell the truth' – Palestinian saying.

This is the bread of the Arab lands, also known as pita, Syrian bread and bideh. Khubz Arabi is the ideal bread for eating with most Arab foods. It is a flat bread which is hollow and this makes a fine sandwich into which kebabs, salads and other foods can be stuffed. Bread is eaten with every meal and indeed one wonders, seeing all the bread that is consumed, which is the main course – the meat, the vegetables or the bread. It is not surprising that Middle Eastern people do not have special names for lunch and dinner, instead they use the expression 'to eat bread'. Bread is the staff of life and although today in the cities people purchase their loaves from bakeries, in the country villages the women prepare their own dough which they then take to the bakeries to be cooked. In my grandfather's bakery I recall children used to bring their family dough in large copper containers to be prepared and baked. And believe me there is nothing tastier than freshly baked bread straight from a wood-fired oven. Nowadays Arab bread, or pita as it is known in the West, can be easily bought from all continental, Greek and most Indian shops.

Khubz Arabi is not very difficult to prepare and the following recipe will make about 8 loaves.

15 g (½ oz) fresh yeast, or 8 g (¼ oz) dried yeast
About 300 ml (½ pint) tepid water
Pinch of sugar
450 g (1 lb) plain flour
½ teaspoon salt
Oil

1 In a small bowl dissolve the yeast in about 3–4 tablespoons of the water.
2 Stir in the sugar and leave in a warm place for 10–15 minutes or until it becomes frothy.
3 Sift the flour and salt into a warmed mixing bowl.
4 Make a well in the centre and pour in the yeast mixture.
5 Add enough tepid water to make a firm, but not hard, dough.
6 Lightly flour a working surface and knead the dough on

it for about 15 minutes until it is smooth and elastic and no longer sticks to your hands.

7 If you knead in a tablespoon of oil it will make a softer bread.

8 Wash and dry the mixing bowl and oil it.

9 Roll the dough round and round the bowl until it is greased all over – this will prevent the dough from going crusty and cracking while rising.

10 Cover the bowl with a damp cloth and leave in a warm place for at least 2 hours when it should have almost doubled in size.

11 Punch it down and knead for a few minutes.

12 Divide the mixture into 6 or 8 pieces depending on the size of pita you want.

13 Roll them in the hands until they are round and smooth.

14 Lightly flour a board and flatten out each round on it with the palm of your hand, or with a rolling pin, until it is about 5 mm (¼ in) thick and is as even and as circular as possible.

15 Dust the rounds with flour and cover with a cloth. Leave to rise in a warm place for 20–30 minutes.

16 Preheat the oven to 230-240°C (450-475°F, Gas Mark 8/9), putting in two large oiled baking sheets halfway through the heating period.

17 When the oven is ready slide the rounds of dough on to the hot sheets, dampening the tops to prevent them browning, and bake for 10 minutes.

18 Do not open the oven door during this time; after 10 minutes open it cautiously to see if the pitas have puffed up.

19 Put on to wire racks to cool as soon as you remove them from the oven. They should be soft and white with a pouch inside.

6–8 pitas

MANNAEESH
Thyme bread

A Lebanese favourite Mannaeesh Zahtar, as it is sometimes called, is one of those Middle Eastern specialities that is as old as time. Mannaeesh is sold in small shops at street corners or is piled sky-high on the head of a street vendor.

There are several versions of this bread. It comes round, as in this recipe, half-moon-shaped or – and this is my personal favourite – a hollowed round bread called Kaahk Mannaeesh.

To eat mannaeesh first break it and sprinkle the inside with zahtar (see page 56) which is basically the same mixture of herbs and spices as in mannaeesh. Then you can munch and crunch your way through the labyrinthine streets of Beirut or Tripoli!

It is an unusual bread which is ideal for breakfast or afternoon tea.

450 g (1 lb) plain flour
15 g (½ oz) fresh yeast, or 8 g (¼ oz) dried yeast
½ teaspoon salt
Pinch sugar
5–6 tablespoons olive oil
15 g (½ oz) dried thyme
8 g (¼ oz) dried marjoram
3 tablespoons sesame seeds

1 Prepare the dough as for khubz Arabi (see page 227) and when it is ready divide it into 10 or more portions.
2 Roll each portion between your palms until it is smooth and round.
3 Flour a board and flatten each one with a rolling pin until it is circular, even, and about 5 mm (¼ in) thick.
4 Leave in a warm place for 20 minutes.
5 Brush the tops of the rounds with olive oil.

6 Mix the oil, thyme, marjoram and sesame seeds together in a small bowl.

7 Spread this mixture all over the surface of each round.

8 Pre-heat the oven to 230°C (450°F, Gas Mark 8), putting in two large, oiled baking sheets halfway through the heating period.

9 Slide the mannaeesh rounds on to the hot sheets and bake for 8–10 minutes.

10 Remove from the oven and put on to wire racks to cool. The bread should be soft.

About 10 large baps

KHUBZ BASALI
Onion bread

The ancient Cappadocians and Cilicians were famed for their breads. They were also the ancestors of the present-day Syrians and some of the Armenians and Turks. It is therefore not surprising to find this very unusual bread in the repertoire of the north Syrian cuisine. Its origins are very old, but what we do know is that the peoples of Antioch (Antakya), Aleppo and Cilician Armenia have been baking and eating it throughout the centuries.

This bread is often prepared in small rounds very much like khubz Arabi (see page 227), but the recipe below is for a whole loaf. It is wonderful for breakfast or, as often eaten by the Syrians, with hard-boiled eggs, laban, cheese and fresh raw vegetables.

225 g (8 oz) self-raising flour
½ teaspoon salt
1 teaspoon baking powder
½ teaspoon cumin
½ teaspoon thyme
¼ teaspoon chilli pepper

10 black olives, seeded and coarsely chopped
1 small onion, finely chopped
4–5 tablespoons oil, olive or groundnut
Water – 300 ml (½ pint) or slightly less

1 Sift the flour and salt into a warmed mixing bowl.
2 Make a well in the centre and add the water to make a firm, but not hard, dough.
3 Add the baking powder, cumin, thyme, chilli pepper, salt, chopped olives and onion.
4 Lightly flour a working surface and knead the dough on it for about 15 minutes until it is smooth and elastic and no longer sticks to your hands.
5 Add the oil and knead well. This will not only help to give the bread its particular taste, but will also soften it.
6 Wash and dry the mixing bowl and lightly oil it.
7 Roll the dough round and round the bowl until it is greased all over – this will prevent the dough from going crusty and cracking while rising.
8 Place the dough in a greased bread tin, cover with a damp cloth and leave it in a warm place for about ½ hour to rise.
9 Bake in an oven preheated to 180°C (350°F, Gas Mark 4) for 45–50 minutes until the crust is golden brown.
10 Remove from the baking tin, cool and serve.

1 loaf

KHUBZ SAJ
Thin bread

The price of small commodities is, at this mid-way station, five to eight times the market worth at Damascus. The Jurdy have brought down Syrian olives, leeks and cheese and caravan biscuit. The Jurdy baker was busy with his fire-pit of sticks in the earth and his girdle pans, 'tannar', to make fine white flat bread for the pennies of the poor pilgrims. The refreshing sweet and sour lemons and halweh dates from el-Ally, I saw very soon sold out.

Arabia Deserta

If khubz Arabi, pita bread, is the bread of the city-dwelling Arabs then khubz saj is that of the village and nomadic Arabs. This form of bread is probably the oldest found in the Middle East. It is still prepared in the menzils (camping sites of the nomads and caravans) with a fire of dry sticks and camel dung. Saj is a domed oven made of cast iron with the wood burning underneath. When I was a child in Lebanon we used to go up the hills to collect pine needles scattered on the ground in their millions. Laden with sackfuls of these we descended to our homes and stored the pine needles – which incidentally make excellent firewood giving a magnificent glow – so that twice a week the old women could bake the khubz saj. They did this by flattening the dough until very thin, arranging the dough on a specially made round pillow with a band where the hand would grip the back of the pillow. Then, quick as a flash, the pillow was thrown on to the hot cast iron oven and, just as quickly, the bread was withdrawn. The whole baking procedure does not last more than a minute or so. The breads are stacked one on top of the other. At one session I recall over 200 thin breads being made. The breads were then distributed amongst the families concerned.

Below is a simplified version of khubz saj which is marvellous with kebabs or any mezzeh dip. My favourite way of eating it is to arrange a kebab and salad over half of it and then to roll it up and eat it like a sandwich.

25 g (1 oz) fresh yeast, or 15 g (½ oz) dried yeast
Lukewarm water
1 teaspoon sugar

1·5 kg (3 lb) plain flour
2 teaspoons salt

1 Dissolve the yeast in 600 ml (1 pint) warm water.
2 Stir in the sugar.
3 Sift the flour and salt into a large mixing bowl.
4 Make a well in the centre of the flour and slowly work in the
   dissolved yeast mixture and enough warm water to make a
   stiff dough.
5 Knead well on a floured surface for about 10 minutes.
6 Place the ball of dough in a clean bowl, cover with a cloth and
   leave in a warm place for about 3 hours.
7 Transfer the dough to a floured surface, punch it down and
   knead for a few minutes.
8 Leave it in the bowl, covered, for a further 30 minutes.
9 Flour the working surface again.
10 Divide the dough into balls about the size of a medium-sized
   apple, producing about 30 balls.
11 With a long rolling pin roll out each ball into a thin sheet about
   25 cm (10 in) in diameter.
12 Line the bottom of the oven with aluminium foil.
13 Heat the oven to 200°C (400°F, Gas Mark 6).
14 Place a sheet of dough on the foil and cook for about 3 minutes.
15 Remove, cover with a cloth to keep warm, and continue the
   baking process until all 30 are cooked.
16 Serve immediately while hot.

NB Although absolutely delicious when fresh, they can also be
    successfully stored in a freezer. When you wish to serve them,
    first defrost, sprinkle lightly with water, wrap in a teatowel
    and leave for 10 minutes to absorb the moisture and to soften.

Makes 30 pieces

KHUBZ TABOUN
Mosaic bread

'His bread is kneaded and his water is in the jug'– refers to a man who has everything.

A fascinating bread from Arabia and Iraq similar to the Iranian coarse bread called sang-gak which is baked on hot pebbles or stones. This method of cooking is understandable as the nomads often had no resources or cooking utensils and were obliged to improvise.

Khubz Taboun is nowadays baked and sold in small shops. Each bread is about 1 metre (1 yard) long, but is usually sold in strips. Khubz Taboun really does have a unique flavour. I have never been quite sure why except that perhaps it is the earthy, rocky taste and also its irregular shape.

Below is a simplified version adapted to suit modern ovens. Next time you are at the seaside start collecting pebbles or stones for making this unusual bread.

450 g (1 lb) wholewheat flour
15 g (½ oz) fresh yeast, or 8 g (¼ oz) dried yeast
300 ml (½ pint) tepid water
½ teaspoon salt
1 tablespoon sugar

1 Follow the same preparation procedure as for khubz Arabi (see page 227) and when the dough is ready divide it into 4 portions.
2 Meanwhile place pebbles about 5 cm (2 in) or more in size on the bottom of the oven.
3 Heat the oven to 230°C (450°F, Gas Mark 8) and leave for 1 hour until the pebbles are very hot to the touch.
4 Now flour a board and flatten each ball of dough with a rolling pin until it is about 5 mm (¼ in) thick.
5 Dust the dough rounds with flour and cover with a cloth.
6 Leave in a warm place for about 30 minutes.

7 Once satisfied that the pebbles are hot, lower the heat to 110°C (225°F, Gas Mark ¼).

8 Very carefully place each dough round on the hot pebbles.

9 Bake for 50–60 minutes at the low heat until the bread is golden brown.

10 Remove the bread from the oven to cool. The loaves will be an irregular shape and have an individual taste.

Makes 4 loaves

LABAN
Yogourt

'The housewives spread the tent-cloths, taking out the corner and side-cords; and finding some wild stone for a hammer, they beat down their tent pegs into the ground, and under-setting the tent stakes or "pillars" (am'dan) they heave and stretch the tent-cloth: and now their booths are standing. The wife enters, and when she has bestowed her stuff, she brings forth the man's breakfast; that is a bowl of leban, poured from the soured milk-skin, or it is a clot of dates with a bowl of the desert water: for guest-days it is dates and buttermilk with a piece of sweet butter. After that she sits within, rocking upon her knees the "semila" or sour milk-skin, to make this day's butter.'

Arabia Deserta

Yogourt is an essential ingredient in Middle Eastern cooking in general, but is not so common in Arab cooking. In al-Baghdadi's medieval manual yogourt was referred to as 'Persian milk' and, indeed, it originates via the Iranian peoples from the Aryan races that overran the Middle East over 10,000 years ago.

Today yogourt is still more popular with the Iranian, Kurdish and Armenian peoples and through them it was passed on to the Arabs, Turks and the Balkan lands. It is certainly not of Turkish origin, nor Greek, Bulgarian or Arab. Of the dishes utilizing yogourt in the Arabic cuisine, the majority are found in Syria, Lebanon and northern Iraq where the Armenian and Kurdish influences have been strong.

Yogourt contains beneficial bacteria that work like yeast. A little, when added to warm milk, will help the bacteria (*lacto bacillus Bulgaricus*) to grow and multiply. Fresh, live yogourt can now be bought in most food stores, but I suggest that you make your own – not only is it cheaper, but also much tastier.

    1·2 litres (2 pints) milk
    1 tablespoon live yogourt – called 'starter'

1 Pour the milk into a saucepan and bring it to the boil.
2 As the froth rises turn off the heat.
3 Allow the milk to cool to the point where you can dip your finger in and count up to 15 without screaming!
4 Put one tablespoon of the 'starter' into a cup, add 2 or 3 tablespoons of the warm milk and beat until smooth.
5 Pour this mixture back into the saucepan and stir carefully.
6 Pour the milk into a bowl, cover with a large plate and then wrap a teatowel around the bowl.
7 Place in a warm place, eg near a radiator or fireplace or in the airing cupboard, and leave for about 8 hours or overnight.
8 Transfer the bowl to the refrigerator.
9 Yogourt can be kept for up to a week in the refrigerator before it starts to turn sour. When it is near to finishing use a little as the new 'starter' to make more yogourt.

Makes 1·2 litres (2 pints)

STABILISED YOGOURT

If you are to use yogourt in hot dishes eg sauces, soups or stews, it is necessary to stabilize it first or else it will curdle. To do this you can either

a) Stir 1 tablespoon of flour into a little water until you have a smooth paste and then stir it into the yogourt before you heat it or

b) Beat an egg into the yogourt before cooking.

Sweets

HALAWAH TEMAR	*Date halva*
MAMOUNIA	*Aleppan halva*
BASBOUSA-BIL-JOZ-EL-HINDI	*Halva with coconut*
HALAWAH-BIL-LOZ	*Halva with almonds*
MA-MOUL	*Stuffed Easter pastries*
KARABIJ	*Stuffed pastries with natife*
GHORAYEBAH	*Lover's shortbread*
MAHLEBIEH	*Ground rice pudding*
PORTUKHAL MAHLEBIEH	*Orange custard*
ASABEH-EL-ARUSS	*Bride's fingers*
BAKLAWA	*Flaky pastry with nuts and syrup*
KUNAFAH	*Shredded pastry with nuts and syrup*
BALOURIEH	*White kunafah*
BARAZEH SHAMI	*Damascus sesame biscuits*
SALATAH FAOWAKEH	*Fruit salad*
AWAMYMAT	*Epiphany doughnut balls*
MSHABBAK	*Patterned doughnuts*
SOUARZEH	*Bird's nest pastries*

HALAWAH TEMAR
Date halva

If the Turks have Rahat Lokum (Turkish delight) then the Iraqis have two sweets. One is called Manana and the other Halawah Temar. The latter is a very simple sweet, takes only a few minutes to make and is very, very sweet. Dates, of course, are the basic fruit of the land and so understandably appear wherever possible in the local cuisine. You can vary the proportions and variety of the nuts, but by far the most popular is this recipe using half walnuts and half almonds. You can also purchase Iraqi dates stuffed with walnuts or almonds from Middle Eastern shops and these are excellent in this recipe.

450 g (1 lb) dates, stoned and chopped
225 g (½ lb) walnuts, shelled and coarsely chopped
225 g (½ lb) almonds, coarsely chopped
Icing sugar

1 Mix the dates and nuts together in a large bowl and knead until smooth.
2 Lightly dust a board with icing sugar.
3 Place the ball of dates and nuts on the board and with a rolling pin dusted with icing sugar roll it out into a square about 1–1·5 cm (½–¾ in) thick.
4 With a sharp knife cut into 2·5 cm (1 in) squares.
5 Dust a serving plate with icing sugar, arrange the squares on it and dust with a little more icing sugar.
6 Serve with double or, preferably, clotted cream.

Makes about 40 pieces, but will keep for weeks in a tin

MAMOUNIA
Aleppan halva

This sweet is named after the great Khalif Mamoon, who was
the son of the even more famed Haroun-al-Rasheed of
Baghdad. Interestingly enough this sweet is almost unknown
in Baghdad and is, in fact, the speciality of Aleppo in
northern Syria. It is eaten daily for breakfast, and I recall
seeing people queueing up in the mornings on their way to
work to eat a plateful of mamounia in those colourfully ramshackle small shops of Aleppo.

There are many variations of mamounia. The recipe
below is a typical one popular with my family, many of them
still living in Aleppo. Some people pour doubled or clotted
cream over the mamounia; I personally prefer mine plain,
but perhaps when served as a dessert, as it often is, a little
cream is acceptable.

    100 g (4 oz) unsalted butter
    100 g (4 oz) semolina
    1 teaspoon ground cinnamon
    Syrup
    600 ml (1 pint) water
    175 g (6 oz) sugar
    1 tablespoon lemon juice

1 First make the syrup (which is called eishta in Arabic) by
   putting the water, sugar and lemon juice into a saucepan
   and bringing to the boil.
2 Lower the heat and simmer for 10 minutes then remove
   from the heat and set aside.
3 In a large saucepan melt the butter.
4 Add the semolina and fry, stirring constanty, for about 5
   minutes or until the sweet becomes crumbly in appearance.
5 Pour in the syrup and mix thoroughly with a wooden
   spoon.
6 Cook for another 2–3 minutes.

7 Remove from the heat and set aside for 12–15 minutes.
8 Spoon into a serving bowl, sprinkle with the cinnamon
   and serve while still warm.

6 servings

BASBOUSA-BIL-JOZ-EL-HINDI
Halva with coconut

Helweh means sweet in Arabic and from that come desserts
named halawah or halva in Turkish. In Egypt halawah
dishes are often known as basbousa. All halawah dishes were
once made with rice, but that has now been replaced by
semolina, or simit – as it is known in Armenian and Turkish.

Basbousa with coconut is a particular favourite in Egypt.
Coconut is not very widespread in Arabic cooking and,
understandably enough, it only appears in the Middle East
in Iran and in the Arabian Gulf regions. Therefore I suspect
that the use of coconut in Egyptian cooking came via the
Mameluks who were originally soldiers of fortune of
Turkish, Caucasian and Persian origin and who ruled Egypt
for several centuries from about 1250–1517.

This recipe can be served hot or cold, although I prefer the
latter. It is traditionally cut into lozenge shapes.

   50 g (2 oz) plain flour
   1 teaspoon baking powder
   350 g (12 oz) semolina
   225 g (8 oz) castor sugar
   50 g (2 oz) desiccated coconut
   100 g (4 oz) unsalted butter, melted
   250 ml (8 fl oz) milk
   1 teaspoon vanilla essence
   $1\frac{1}{2}$ teaspoons ground cinnamon

Syrup
225 g (8 oz) sugar
150 ml (¼ pint) water
1 tablespoon lemon juice

1　To prepare the syrup, place the sugar, water and lemon juice in a saucepan and bring to the boil.
2　Simmer for 6–8 minutes until the syrup is thick.
3　Remove from the heat, cool and then refrigerate.
4　Sieve the flour and baking powder into a large bowl.
5　Add the semolina, sugar and coconut and mix well.
6　Pour in the melted butter, milk and vanilla essence and stir until completely mixed.
7　Stir in 1 teaspoon of the cinnamon.
8　Spoon this mixture into a greased tin measuring about 28 × 18 cm (11 × 7 in) so that it is about 1 cm (½ in) thick.
9　Sprinkle the remaining ½ teaspoon of cinnamon over the top.
10　Bake in an oven preheated to 170°C (325°F, Gas Mark 3) for about 30–40 minutes until the top is crisp and golden brown.
11　Remove from the oven and cut into lozenge shapes.
12　Quickly pour the cold syrup over the basbousa.
13　Serve hot or cold, with a little double cream if liked.

8–10 servings

HALAWAH-BIL-LOZ
Halva with almonds

'At last, as midday approached with its stifling heat, something floating on the surface of the water caught his eyes. It seemed like a mass of leaves wrapped up with fibre, and wading into the river he succeeded in catching it . . . it contained a quantity of the most delicious-looking halwa, that famous marzipan of the making of which only Baghdad knows the secret, a sweetmeat composed of sugar mingled with almonds and attar of roses and other delicate and savoury essences . . .'

'The Food of Paradise' – Ibn Amjed

600 ml (1 pint) water
350 g (12 oz) sugar
1½ teaspoons lemon juice
1 teaspoon rosewater
100 g (4 oz) blanched almonds
100 g (4 oz) unsalted butter
175 g (6 oz) semolina
2 tablespoons raisins
Garnish
Whole almonds
Whipped double cream – optional

1 Place the water, sugar and lemon juice in a saucepan and bring to the boil.
2 Simmer for about 5 minutes and then remove from the heat and stir in the rosewater.
3 Chop the almonds finely.
4 Melt the butter in a large saucepan, add the almonds, semolina and raisins and fry, stirring constantly, until golden in colour.
5 Now add the hot syrup to the semolina mixture slowly, stirring constantly, until the mixture thickens – about 3–5 minutes.
6 Remove from the heat and cover; leave to cool for about 10 minutes.
7 Pour it into small dessert dishes and flatten the tops.
8 Decorate with a few whole almonds and serve as it is or with some whipped cream.

6 servings

MA-MOUL
Stuffed Easter pastries

Ma-moul is a speciality of Aleppo. I do not mean the present city of that name, but more the region 'Sanjak of Aleppo' which covered very large areas of Syria and Turkey in the hey-day of the Ottoman Empire. It is important to note this geographical fact since there are many dishes which emanate from Syria but are not Syrian by origin.

Ma-moul was traditionally baked at Easter time – naturally by the Christians of Aleppo who were, by and large, Greek Orthodox, Maronite, Assyrian and Armenian. Nowadays it is sold all the year round in good quality sweet shops of the Middle East, especially in Aleppo, Damascus, Beirut and Amman.

Ma-mouls are stuffed pastries covered with icing sugar. The actual ingredients vary from region to region. The Aleppans prefer walnuts and almonds; the Armenians use dates and walnuts; the Lebanese like walnuts and pistachio nuts, and prefer to use semolina instead of flour.

Below is a family recipe which uses dates, walnuts and almonds.

Filling
225 g (½ lb) stoned dates
100 g (¼ lb) walnuts, roughly chopped
100 g (¼ lb) almonds, roughly chopped (you can use
   pistachio nuts instead)
150 ml (¼ pint) water
100 g (¼ lb) sugar
1 heaped teaspoon cinnamon
Dough
450 g (1 lb) plain flour
225 g (½ lb) unsalted butter, melted
2 tablespoons rosewater

4–5 tablespoons milk
Sifted icing sugar

1 First prepare the filling. Chop the dates and place them with the chopped nuts into a saucepan together with the water, sugar and cinnamon.

2 Cook over a low heat until the dates are soft and the water has been absorbed.

3 Sift the flour into a bowl, add the melted butter and mix by hand.

4 Add the rosewater and milk and knead the dough until it is soft and easy to mould.

5 Divide the dough into walnut-sized lumps.

6 Take one lump, roll it into a ball between your palms and then hollow it out with your thumb, pinching the sides up until they are thin and form a pot shape.

7 Now fill the pot with some of the date mixture and then press the dough back over the filling to make a ball.

8 Gently press with your palm to slightly flatten it or, if you have a wooden spoon with a deep, carved bowl, use it to mould each pastry.

9 Repeat the procedure until you have used all the pastry and filling.

10 Arrange the pastries on baking sheets.

11 Make interesting patterns with a fork on each pastry. The traditional one is to make straight lines down the length of each pastry.

12 Place in an oven preheated to 150°C (300°F, Gas Mark 2) for about 30 minutes. Do not let them change colour or they will become hard.

13 Remove from the oven and allow to cool.

14 When cold roll them in the icing sugar.

15 Store in an airtight tin.

Makes 30 pastries

KARABIJ
Stuffed pastries with natife

Another of those famed specialities of Aleppo, karabij is a
pastry similar to Ma-moul, but often a little smaller in size.
These stuffed pastries are dipped in a cream called natife
before being eaten. The distinctive flavour of the cream
comes from small pieces of wood known in Arabic as erh
halawah (the soul of the sweets). It is better known in Europe
as bois de Panama. I have found this aromatic wood in
health food shops and in some Middle Eastern stores. The
Greeks call it halawah wood. It sometimes comes in
powdered form which should make your task easier. I recall
my father telling me that the hills of Cilicia were abundant
with this shrub-like tree, and that it was one of the great
exporting commodities of that region.

You will not find karabij sold in the shops. It is a speciality
of the home and then often only on very special occasions, eg
birthdays, weddings, Christmas etc. Like Ma-moul, Karabij
is of pre-Muslim origin and I would like to think it is even
pre-Byzantine, but whatever its history it is one of the most
original of Middle Eastern sweets. It is a unique pastry in the
'land of pastries'.

Cream
75 g (3 oz) erh halawa (halawa wood)
225 g (½ lb) sugar
1 tablespoon lemon juice
2 tablespoons orange blossom water
4 egg whites
Filling
225 g (½ lb) walnuts, finely chopped
100 g (¼ lb) sugar
1 tablespoon cinnamon
Dough
450 g (1 lb) plain flour

225 g (½ lb) unsalted butter, melted
3–4 tablespoons water

1 First prepare the cream by pulverizing the piece of erh halawa.
2 Place in a bowl with about 150 ml (¼ pint) water and leave to soak for 4–5 hours.
3 Transfer the contents of the bowl to a saucepan, bring to the boil, lower the heat and simmer until the liquid has thickened.
4 Strain the mixture through fine muslin and set the liquid aside while you prepare the syrup.
5 Now dissolve the sugar in 8 tablespoons of water, add the lemon juice and bring to the boil.
6 Lower the heat and simmer until the syrup has thickened – about 10 minutes.
7 Remove from the heat, stir in the orange blossom water and the hot thickened erh halawa; stir vigorously and set aside to cool.
8 When the mixture is cold place the egg whites in a large bowl and whisk until they are very stiff. Use an electric whisk if you have one.
9 Now very gradually add the cold syrup mixture, beating continuously until the mixture froths and expands. Again you can use an electric whisk.
10 Transfer to a serving dish and set aside until ready to use.
11 Make the filling by mixing together in a bowl the chopped nuts, sugar and cinnamon.
12 To make the dough, first sift the flour into a large bowl, add the melted butter and mix by hand.
13 Add the water and knead until the dough is soft and easy to mould. Add a little more water if necessary.
14 Divide the dough into walnut-sized lumps.
15 Take one lump, roll it into a ball between the palms and then hollow it out with your thumb, pinching the sides up

until they are thin and form a pot shape.

16 Fill the pot with a little of the nut mixture and then press the dough back over the filling to form a ball.

17 Gently press between your palms to make a small oval shape.

18 Repeat the procedure until you have used up all the dough and filling.

19 Place the karabij on baking trays and cook in an oven preheated to 150°C (300°F, Gas Mark 2) for 20–25 minutes. Remove from the oven before they start to change colour.

20 Set aside to cool.

21 When serving arrange the karabij on a large dish and accompany them with a bowl of the natife cream, into which the pastries are dipped.

22 Both the pastries and the cream will keep for a long time.

Makes 30 pastries

GHORAYEBAH
Lover's shortbread

'For those in love . . .
    Love is simple as Ghorayebah.
    Love is fragrant as Ghorayebah.
    Love melts gently as Ghorayebah.
For those in love.'

Traditional Syrian song

These are delicious pastries that literally melt in the mouth. A Syrian speciality, these biscuits appear throughout the Middle East in some shape or other. They are simple to make and delightful with tea or coffee.

    450 g (1 lb) butter
    225 g (8 oz) icing sugar, sifted

450 g (1 lb) plain flour, sifted
Blanched almonds

1 Melt the butter in a small saucepan over a low heat.
2 Spoon off any froth and pour the yellow liquid into a large mixing bowl, discarding any salt residue and water left in the pan.
3 Put the bowl in the refrigerator and leave until the butter has solidified.
4 Beat or whisk the butter until it is white and creamy.
5 Add the icing sugar, a little at a time, and continue beating.
6 Add the flour, a little at a time, and continue to mix until the mixture is stiff.
7 Collect the dough up and knead it by hand until it forms a ball and becomes smooth and pliable.
8 Leave to rest in the bowl for about 10 minutes.
9 Preheat the oven to 150°C (300°F, Gas Mark 2).
10 On a clean working surface shape the dough mixture into small balls about the size of a walnut.
11 Roll each one into a sausage and then join the ends to make a circle.
12 Place an almond over the join.
13 Lay the ghorayebah on baking trays, leaving about a 2·5 cm (1 in) space between each one.
14 Place in the oven and cook for about 20 minutes or until the almonds are a very light golden brown, but the biscuits are still white.

Makes about 35 biscuits

MAHLEBIEH
Ground rice pudding

This is a rice pudding with a difference; simple yet highly sophisticated, it is popular throughout the Arab lands.

Always served chilled it is often decorated with chopped pistachio nuts which give the pudding a touch of colour. Chopped almonds or a syrup made of honey and water scented with orange blossom water is also often added to the top of the cold Mahlebieh – which literally translates as 'with milk'.

I personally prefer to top the pudding with a mixture of chopped pistachios and pomegranate seeds, not only from a decorative point of view, but because the lightly pungent taste of the pomegranate offsets the sweetness of the Mahlebieh.

100g (4 oz) ground rice
2 level tablespoons cornflour
1·2 litres (2 pints) milk
8 tablespoons sugar
2 tablespoons orange blossom water, or rose water, or a
   mixture of the two
¼ teaspoon grated nutmeg
100 g (4 oz) ground almonds
1 small pomegranate, seeded
2 tablespoons chopped pistachio nuts

1 In a large bowl mix together the rice and cornflour.
2 Add about 10 tablespoons of the cold milk and stir until
   you have a smooth paste.
3 Bring the rest of the milk to the boil in a large saucepan.
4 Add the sugar and stir until it is dissolved.
5 Slowly pour the hot milk on to the rice paste, stirring
   constantly.
6 Pour the mixture back into the saucepan and cook over a
   low heat, stirring constantly, until the mixture thickens.
7 Stir in the orange or rose water and the nutmeg and cook
   for a further 3–4 minutes, stirring constantly.
8 Remove from the heat and stir in the almonds.

9 Pour into a serving bowl, leave to cool and then place in the refrigerator to chill.

10 Before serving decorate with the pomegranate seeds and pistachio nuts.

6 servings

PORTUKHAL MAHLEBIEH
Orange custard

This is a delicate and delicious sweet from Beirut which has European influences. Lebanon, of course, is famed for her orange groves but, unfortunately with the desire to industrialize, these have dwindled over the years almost into insignificance. So much so that when there I was served Spanish and Moroccan oranges instead of their local 'Antilias' produce, my host informed me that most of the beautiful groves had been sacrificed to motorways and residential blocks to satisfy a money-hungry society. The need to ape the West has unfortunately affected the Lebanese cuisine which seems to take a delight in casting aside its true Middle Eastern heritage and adopting that of the West – often not very successfully.

3 eggs
4 tablespoons castor sugar
¼ teaspoon salt
450 ml (¾ pint) milk, scalded
1 teaspoon vanilla essence
4 oranges
100 g (¼ lb) granulated sugar
2 tablespoons hot water
1 teaspoon cinnamon
1 tablespoon finely chopped pistachio nuts

1 Beat the eggs and mix with the castor sugar in the top of a double boiler or in a bowl which will fit over a saucepan.

2 Gradually stir in the salt and scalded milk.

3 Now put the pan or bowl over a pan of boiling water and, stirring constantly, cook for 10–15 minutes or until the custard thickens.

4 Remove the pan or bowl containing the custard and place in a bowl containing a little cold water to cool.

5 Stir in the vanilla essence.

6 Meanwhile peel and slice the oranges crossways into slices 5 mm (¼ in) thick.

7 Arrange the slices over the base of a shallow glass serving dish.

8 When the custard is cold beat it well with a wooden spoon.

9 Pour the custard over the orange slices.

10 Heat the granulated sugar in a small saucepan until it melts, add the 2 tablespoons hot water, stir well and cook for about 2 minutes and then immediately pour over the custard.

11 Sprinkle with the cinnamon and chopped pistachio nuts and serve.

6 servings

ASABEH-EL-ARUSS
Bride's fingers

This is a traditional recipe that also appears in medieval manuscripts as lauzinaj. They are cigar-shaped sweets in which an almond filling is wrapped in paper-thin pastry and then dipped in syrup. The medieval recipes recommended frying them and dusting with castor sugar. In some areas of the Middle East, especially Syria and Lebanon, crushed pistachios are used instead of almonds. Although bride's fingers have much the same ingredients as the more celebrated baklawa they are simpler to make and lighter to eat.

I have included a recipe for syrup, should you wish to use it – otherwise use castor sugar.

225 g (½ lb) almonds or pistachio nuts, coarsely ground
2 teaspoons cinnamon
2 teaspoons sugar
225 g (½ lb) unsalted butter
450 g (1 lb) fillo pastry (can be purchased in most Middle Eastern delicatessens)
Syrup
350 g (12 oz [2 teacups]) sugar
350 ml (12 fl oz [1½ teacups]) water
Juice of 1 lemon
2 tablespoons rosewater

1 If using syrup make this first by putting the sugar, water and lemon juice into a saucepan.
2 Bring to the boil, lower the heat and simmer until the syrup leaves a sticky film on a spoon.
3 Add the rosewater and set aside to cool.
4 To make the fingers, first mix together in a bowl the nuts, cinnamon and sugar.
5 Melt the butter in a small saucepan over a low heat.
6 Brush a baking sheet with a little of the melted butter.
7 Open out the fillo pastry and cut along the fold so that each sheet is divided into two rectangles.
8 While you are using each sheet of pastry keep the others covered or they will become dry and brittle.
9 Lay a rectangle of pastry on a working top, short side nearest you, and brush the two long edges with butter.
10 Arrange 1 teaspoon of the nut mixture in a ridge across the short side nearest you.
11 Fold the two long sides inwards, over the ends of the almond mixture. Then roll up the pastry from the short

side nearer you over the nut mixture, and on to the short
side away from you (to form a cigar shape).

12 Place each roll on the baking sheet.
13 Brush them all with the remaining melted butter.
14 Cook in an oven preheated to 190°C (375°F, Gas Mark 5)
for 20–30 minutes or until golden brown.
15 Either dip the hot fingers into the cold syrup and then
arrange on a serving dish, or dredge the fingers with the
castor sugar and serve.

Makes about 40 'fingers'

BAKLAWA
Flaky pastry with nuts and syrup

> *Syrup*
> 350 g (12 oz) sugar
> 350 ml (12 fl oz) water
> 1 tablespoon lemon juice
> 2 tablespoons rosewater
> *Pastry*
> 1 packet (450 g [1 lb]) fillo pastry
> 225 g (½ lb) unsalted butter
> 225 g (½ lb) walnuts, chopped or coarsely ground

1 First make the syrup by putting the sugar, water and
lemon juice in a saucepan and bringing to the boil.
2 Lower the heat and simmer for about 10 minutes or until
the syrup leaves a slightly sticky film on a spoon.
3 Add the rosewater and set aside to cool.
4 When making baklawa a slight problem arises in respect
of the size of tin to use. Most packets of pastry contain
sheets about 54 × 28 cm (21 × 11 in), but it is not easy to
find a tin with these dimensions. I use one measuring
30 × 20 cm (12 × 8 in), but it is necessary to trim the
sheets to make them fit. As baklawa consists of many

layers of pastry and, as I am loath to waste good food, I simply slip the trimmings between the sheets maintaining an even thickness. The one essential factor is the tin must be at least 2·5 cm (1 in) deep.

5 Melt the butter slowly in a small saucepan and skim off any froth on the surface.

6 Grease the baking tin.

7 Lay 2 sheets of pastry on top of each other in the tray and then dribble a tablespoon of the melted butter over the second sheet.

8 Repeat in this way until you have 6 or 8 sheets in the tin.

9 While you are layering all the sheets of pastry for the baklawa refrain from pressing on them. This ensures that air is trapped between the layers so enabling the pastry to rise.

10 Spread half of the crushed nuts over the last layer.

11 Continue with the layers of pastry and spoonfuls of butter until you have laid down a further 6 to 8 sheets.

12 Spread the remaining nuts over the last sheet of pastry.

13 Continue layering the pastry with spoonfuls of melted butter dribbled over alternate sheets until you have used up all the pastry.

14 Spoon any remaining butter over the last sheet, taking care not to use any of the white residue at the bottom of the saucepan.

15 Lightly brush the butter over the last sheet so that every bit of it is covered with butter.

16 Cut the baklawa into lozenge shapes using a sharp knife and taking care to press as little as possible on the actual baklawa.

17 Place the tin in an oven preheated to 180°C (350°F, Gas Mark 4) and cook for ½ hour.

18 Lower the temperature to 150°C (300°F, Gas Mark 2) and cook for a further hour or until the pastry is just turning pale golden.

19 Set the baklawa aside until it is just warm and then pour
    the cold syrup all along the gaps. There will be a sizzling
    sound as the syrup oozes along.
20 Set aside until completely cold.
21 To serve, run a knife along the gaps again to make sure
    that all the layers are completely cut through.

About 25 pieces

KUNAFAH
Shredded pastry with nuts and syrup

> Kunafah swimming in butter
> Bearded with right vermicelli,
> God has not given my belly
> Half of the words it would utter
> Of Kunafah's sweetness
> And syrup's completeness.
>
> Kunafah lies on the table
> Isled in a sweet brown oil,
> Would I not wonder and toil
> Seventy years to be able
> To eat in Paradise
> Kunafah's subtleties?

> *The Book of 1001 Nights*

There are two famed Eastern sweets made with shredded
pastry – Kunafah and Balourieh. Both, as with most sweets,
are of the north Syrian, pre-Arab, period; most probably
Byzantine-Cappadocian. The Greeks and Turks call Kunafah
Kataif; which is really a mis-nomer since 'ataif' is a
pancake and very Persian in origin. In the Middle East all
these sweets are sold in specialist shops in the major cities,
eg Aleppo, Damascus, Beirut, Amman and Alexandria. The
finest ones come from Aleppo, Syria, and I am always
delighted whenever I meet a friend, or indeed anyone, who
arrives from the Middle East with the inevitable oval-shaped
baklawa and kunafah box under his arm. You can purchase

the pastry for this sweet from most Greek and continental shops. Ask for kataifi fillo.

450 g (1 lb) kunafah pastry (usually 1 packet)
350 g (¾ lb) unsalted butter, melted and with the froth removed
350 g (12 oz) pistachio nuts, whole
3 tablespoons sugar
75 g (3 oz) almonds, finely chopped
Syrup
350 g (12 oz) sugar
350 ml (12 fl oz) water
1 tablespoon orange blossom water
Juice of 1 lemon

1 Make the syrup first by putting the sugar, water and lemon juice into a saucepan and bringing to the boil.
2 Lower the heat and simmer until the syrup begins to leave a sticky film on a spoon.
3 Remove from the heat, stir in the orange blossom water and set aside to cool.
4 Put the pastry into a large bowl and gently ease apart the strands without breaking them.
5 Divide the pastry into 3 portions.
6 Take one of the portions and lay it flat on a clean working top.
7 Flatten it as much as possible with your hands until it is about 8–10 mm (⅜–½ in) thick and then shape it into an oblong approximately 30 × 15 cm (12 × 6 in).
8 With a pastry brush, coat the surface with some of the melted butter.
9 Take a flat stick about 45 cm (18 in) long and 2·5 cm (1 in) wide and lay it diagonally across the flattened pastry.
10 Mix the pistachio nuts with the sugar and chopped almonds and arrange a third of the filling evenly along the stick.

11 Roll the strands of the dough around the stick as tightly as possible.

12 Carefully slide the stick out, leaving the filling inside.

13 Brush melted butter all over the roll of pastry.

14 Prepare the other 2 portions of pastry and filling in the same way.

15 Lightly butter the bottom of a baking tray which should measure about 30 x 20 cm (12 x 8 in).

16 Arrange the 3 pastry rolls in the tin and cook in an oven preheated to 180°C (350°F, Gas Mark 4) for $\frac{1}{2}$ hour.

17 Lower the heat to 150°C (300°F, Gas Mark 2) and cook for a further $1\frac{1}{2}$ hours until the kunafah is golden brown.

18 Remove from the oven and pour the cold syrup over the rolls, turning each one so that it is covered all over with the syrup.

19 Leave to cool and cut each roll into pieces 5–7·5 cm (2–3 in) long.

About 25 pastries

BALOURIEH
White kunafah

This is a Syrian speciality – and particularly Aleppan – though in recent years it has spread (deservedly so) throughout Lebanon, Jordan, Palestine and southern Turkey. It is my personal favourite of all the Middle Eastern pastry sweets and, unfortunately, the most expensive because of all the pistachio filling. The pistachio nuts should be uncooked. They are available from good continental shops and health food stores. The pastry is similar to kataifi fillo which can be found in most continental shops. It normally comes in 450 g (1 lb) packets.

The art of cooking this particular sweet is to keep the pastry white. The secret is to cook it at a low heat and to keep the oven door open. It is a very sweet sweet and thus, regrettably, very fattening. However, it is absolutely delightful either with tea or coffee or as a dessert – perhaps with a little cream.

900 g (2 lb) kataifi fillo
275 g (10 oz) melted, skimmed butter
1 tablespoon clear honey
350 g (¾ lb) pistachio nuts, coarsely chopped
65 g (2½ oz) castor sugar
1 tablespoon cinnamon
Syrup
900 g (2 lb) sugar
900 ml (1½ pints) water
1 tablespoon lemon juice

5 tablespoons very finely chopped pistachio nuts

1 Put the melted butter in the refrigerator until semi-solid.
2 Remove from the fridge, place in a bowl and add the honey.
3 Whisk until the honey–butter mixture begins to foam.
4 Pour the mixture into a baking tray measuring about 35 × 45 cm (14 × 18 in) and at least 2·5 cm (1 in) deep.
5 Open up the 2 packets of fillo and lay the pastry out on a clean working surface. In order to loosen the strands I suggest that you divide the pastry into 4 portions and squeeze each portion between the palms of your hands – as though you are making a snowball – for about 2 minutes.
6 Take 2 sections of the fillo and, without breaking it, gently ease the pastry out spreading it over the bottom of the tray.
7 In a small bowl mix together the coarsely chopped nuts and the sugar and cinnamon.
8 Spread this filling evenly over the pastry in the tin.

9 Gently ease apart the 2 remaining portions of pastry and arrange them evenly over the filling.

10 Press the pastry down firmly and tuck in any strands hanging over the edges of the tin.

11 Place in an oven preheated to 150°C (300°F, Gas Mark 2) and bake for 20 minutes. Keep the door just ajar – this will prevent the balourieh from changing colour.

12 Meanwhile prepare the syrup by placing the sugar, water and lemon juice in a saucepan and bringing to the boil.

13 Boil quite vigorously for 5 minutes then remove from the heat.

14 After the balourieh has been cooking for 20 minutes take it from the oven.

15 Very carefully lift the tray at an angle and pour the butter and honey mixture into a bowl.

16 Now completely cover the sweet with another flat surface, eg a kitchen board or the back of another tray, and turn the balourieh over on to this surface.

17 Very gently and carefully slide the sweet – now bottom side up – back into the tin.

18 Return to the oven and, still keeping the door open, cook for a further 10 minutes.

19 Remove from the oven.

20 Pour the boiling syrup evenly over the surface of the sweet.

21 In order to give a tight and compact appearance to the sweet place an empty tray over it and weight it down with something heavy while the sweet cools.

22 When cold cut into 5 cm (2 in) squares.

23 Sprinkle some of the very finely chopped pistachio nuts over each square and serve.

About 25 pastries

BARAZEH SHAMI
Damascus sesame biscuits

450 g (1 lb) plain flour
225 g (8 oz) castor sugar
175 g (6 oz) butter
$\frac{1}{2}$ teaspoon fresh yeast, or $\frac{1}{4}$ teaspoon dried yeast
1 teaspoon sugar
250 ml (8 fl oz) water
50 g (2 oz) melted butter
225 g (8 oz) sesame seeds

1 Sift the flour into a large bowl and stir in the sugar.
2 Add the butter, cut into small pieces, and rub in until the mixture resembles fine breadcrumbs.
3 Dissolve the yeast and the teaspoon of sugar in a little of the water, warmed, and add it to the flour mixture.
4 Gradually add the remaining water and knead for about 5 minutes until the dough is soft and easy to handle. If necessary add a little more water.
5 Cover the bowl with a cloth and leave in a warm place for about 1 hour or until the dough has risen to about twice its size.
6 Remove the dough from the bowl and place on a lightly floured working top.
7 Punch the dough down and then knead for a further 1–2 minutes.
8 Divide the dough into 2 portions.
9 Sprinkle the working surface with a little more flour and roll out one portion until it is about 5 mm ($\frac{1}{4}$ in) thick.
10 Using a teacup or a 10 cm (4 in) cake cutter cut out as many rounds as possible.
11 Repeat with the remaining portion of pastry.
12 Grease two or three baking trays.
13 Spread the sesame seeds out on a plate.
14 Lightly brush both sides of each biscuit with butter and

then dip into the sesame seeds so that both sides are coated.

15 Arrange on the baking sheets, 2·5 cm (1 in) apart, and bake in an oven preheated to 170°C (325°F, Gas Mark 3) for 20–25 minutes or until the biscuits are golden brown and dry.

16 Remove from the oven, cool completely and store in an airtight tin.

SALATAH FAOWAKEH
Fruit salad

'The year when there is plentiful dates and almonds there is prosperity and long life' – Lebanese saying.

This is a delightful Lebanese fruit salad making use of local fruits. Naturally, fresh figs and dates produce the best results and if they are available it is not necessary to soak them. However, dried fruits can also be used to great effect. In the appropriate season mulberries and tout are often used, but for convenience sake I suggest that you follow this recipe and use any liqueur available. In Lebanon they make a fine orange liqueur similar to a Cypriot one called Filfar which is available in Europe.

60 ml (2 fl oz) of mulberry syrup, orange syrup, Filfar, Kirsch or Cointreau
90 ml (3 fl oz) clear honey
8 dried figs (stalks removed), cut into 1 cm (½ in) pieces
About 15 dried dates, stoned and halved
2 tablespoons whole unblanched hazelnuts
1 tablespoon whole unblanched almonds
1 tablespoon pistachio nuts
300 ml (½ pint) lukewarm water
2 tablespoons rosewater
2 tablespoons raisins or sultanas

1 melon, honeydew or ogen
Garnish
2 tablespoons finely chopped pistachio nuts

1 In a bowl mix together the syrup or liqueur, honey, water
   and rosewater until well blended.
2 Add the figs, dates, hazelnuts, almonds, pistachio nuts
   and raisins or sultanas.
3 Stir and leave in the refrigerator for at least 2 hours.
4 Cut the melon in half and discard the seeds.
5 Either use a small ice-cream scoop and scoop out as much
   of the flesh as possible in the form of small balls or remove
   the flesh and chop into 2·5 cm (1 in) pieces.
6 Add the melon flesh to the fruit salad and mix well.
7 Chill for at least another hour.
8 Serve in individual bowls garnished with the chopped
   pistachio nuts to give added colour.

6 servings

AWAMYMAT
Epiphany doughnut balls

These doughnut balls are popular throughout the Middle
East. They appear with different names. In Palestine and
Jordan as Luqmat el Qadi meaning 'judge's mouthful'. They
are known as Zalabia in Egypt, and Awamymat in Syria and
Lebanon. It is Lokma in Turkey and, as usual with the
Greeks, there is 'des' at the end making Lokumades. They
are most probably of pre-Islamic Syrian origin. Incidentally,
they even appear in the Spanish cuisine – probably introduced by the Syrian Arabs who ruled Andalucia for several
centuries.

All oriental sweet shops boast of their pyramids of
Epiphany doughnuts which, as the name suggests, are specially prepared during Epiphany. They can be eaten hot or

cold, but I prefer them hot and dusted with a little cinnamon.
The basic dough batter is similar to 'Mshabbak', as is the
syrup.

Dough
Ingredients as for Mshabbak (see next recipe) but exclude
   the food colouring
Syrup
Ingredients as for Mshabbak (see next recipe)

Oil for frying
1 tablespoon cinnamon

1 First make the syrup as for Mshabbak and set aside to
   cool.
2 Make the dough as described for Mshabbak.
3 Pour 5 cm (2 in) of oil into a large, deep saucepan and
   heat through until hot.
4 When the dough is ready take a teaspoonful, using a wet
   spoon, and drop it into the oil. Another method is to take
   the dough in one hand and gently squeeze it up between
   thumb and forefinger to form small, walnut-sized balls.
5 Fry a few at a time. The dough balls will rise to the surface shaped like walnuts.
6 Turn them over and remove when golden and crisp.
7 Drain on kitchen paper.
8 Dip them immediately into the cold syrup and lift out
   with a slotted spoon.
9 When they are all cooked arrange them in a pyramid
   shape on a large plate.
10 Sprinkle with the cinnamon and serve while still warm.

30–40 balls. Serves 8–10 people

MSHABBAK
Patterned doughnuts

After 26 years' absence I returned to Beirut, some years ago, at the time of the Civil War. Amid that senseless pillage and devastation, in a dark, small side street I noticed an old man with a home-made cart selling Mshabbak. Unable to speak the language I summoned a young Armenian lad of 8 or 9 asking him if he would order some of that sweet for me.

'Ask yourself,' he answered.

'I don't speak the language,' I replied.

'Why not?'

'I come from another country.'

'Where?'

'England.'

'But you speak Armenian!'

'A little,' I said. 'After all, I am Armenian.'

'Oh, all right then.' And he ordered a few penceworth for me which the old man solemnly wrapped in greaseproof paper and handed to him.

'Here. I bet you don't have Mshabbak in your country,' the boy said, smiling.

'You're right,' I said. 'There is no mshabbak like the mshabbaks in a dark, seedy side street in downtown Beirut.'

And I was right. After a few bites I knew I had never lost that particularly 'mshabbakian' flavour from my lips!

450 g (1 lb) plain flour
½ teaspoon salt
15 g (½ oz) fresh yeast, or 8 g (¼ oz) dried yeast
1 teaspoon sugar
300 ml (½ pint) water
300 ml (½ pint) milk
Food colourings of your choice
Syrup
450 g (1 lb) sugar

450 ml (¾ pint) water
1 tablespoon lemon juice
1 tablespoon orange blossom water
2 tablespoons rosewater

Oil for frying

1 First make the syrup by placing the sugar, water and lemon juice in a saucepan and bringing to the boil
2 Simmer for about 10 minutes or until the mixture is slightly sticky and just coats the back of a spoon.
3 Remove from the heat and stir in the orange blossom water and rosewater.
4 Meanwhile prepare the dough by sifting the flour and salt into a large bowl.
5 Place the yeast and sugar in a bowl, add a little of the water (warmed) and stir until the yeast has dissolved.
6 Leave in a warm place until frothy.
7 Now add the rest of the water and milk to the yeast mixture and beat thoroughly.
8 Gradually add the yeast mixture to the flour and continue beating. The dough should be soft, but not quite a liquid.
9 Cover and leave to rise in a warm place for about 1 hour.
10 To make good mshabbak it is advisable to beat the dough at least once more and then let it rest. I prefer to do it twice so that the final result is a well-fermented, sponge-like dough.
11 Meanwhile pour oil into a large, deep saucepan until it is 5 cm (2 in) deep and heat it through.
12 Decide what colours you are going to use and then divide the dough into the requisite portions.
13 Add a little of your chosen food colouring to each portion and beat well.

14 By now the oil should be hot. Spoon one of the coloured portions of pasty into an icing bag with a 5 mm (¼ in) nozzle and slowly squeeze a thin stream into the oil.

15 You can make any patterns of your choice. Traditional ones are:
   a) intertwining circles
   b) a circle filled with an intertwining design
   c) shapes of your choice or even names etc

16 Fry them until golden brown and then remove with a slotted spoon and drain on kitchen paper.

17 Dip immediately into the cold syrup, remove with a slotted spoon and arrange decoratively on a serving plate.

18 Repeat with the remaining coloured portions of batter, taking care to rinse out the icing bag when changing colours.

19 Serve as a dessert with coffee when cold.

About 20 doughnuts depending on the size

SOUARZEH
Bird's nest pastries

These are small, round pastries made with baklawa fillo. They are extremely light and delicious. The name comes from their shape and because of the finely chopped pistachios that give them a light greenish tinge. They are a Syrian speciality, but also popular in southern Turkey where they are known as Antep Bulbulu (Aintab nightingale).

   10 sheets baklawa fillo
   225 g (½ lb) unsalted butter, melted
   Syrup
   900 g (2 lb) sugar

900 ml (1½ pints) water
1 tablespoon lemon juice
Garnish
6–7 tablespoons very finely chopped pistachio nuts

1 Lay out the sheets of pastry, on top of each other, on a working top.
2 Each sheet is approximately 54 x 28 cm (21 x 11 in). Mark the top one into 6 portions, each about 18 x 14 cm (7 x 5½ in) and then cut down through all the 10 sheets.
3 Stack the 60 pieces of pastry on top of each other and keep soft by covering with a damp cloth.
4 Remove one piece of pastry and brush the top all over with a little melted butter.
5 Roll up the pastry as you would a cigarette so that you have a roll 14 cm (5½ in) long.
6 Carefully bend the roll into a circle and squeeze the two ends of the pastry together. They will stick easily if you dampen your fingers first.
7 Repeat the process with all the remaining pieces of pastry.
8 Brush the outer surfaces of the circles with butter and then arrange them on lightly greased baking trays about 1 cm (½ in) apart.
9 Place in an oven preheated to 170°C (325°F, Gas Mark 3) and bake for 20–25 minutes or until they are just turning a light golden brown.
10 While they are cooking prepare the syrup by placing the sugar, water and lemon juice in a saucepan and bringing to the boil.
11 Boil quite vigorously for about 5 minutes then remove from the heat.
12 When the souarzeh are cooked place them in a large shallow dish, pour the boiling syrup over and leave for 2 hours to cool.

13 Arrange the pastries on a large serving plate and dust
with the chopped pistachio nuts.

Makes about 60 small sweets

Drinks

SOUS	*Liquorice root drink*
CHAY-BI-YANASOUN	*Aniseed tea*
KAHWAH	*Arab coffee*
ASAL-OU-KOUSBARAH	*Coriander honey*
AYTAN or AYRAN	*Yogourt drink*
HALEEB-EL-LOZ	*Almond milk*
SAHLAB	*A milk and resin drink*

SOUS
Liquorice root drink

> 'Come on lads let's to the fields
> Shush! let no one hear, to the fields.
> We'll crawl under fences, jump over rocks,
> We'll steal sous make a cool drink.
> Sous! Sous! Sous!
> Allah is great
> God is mighty
> But sous is free and is everyone's!
>
> Childhood song

One of the most memorable events of my childhood which I still recall with a glint of joy was the occasional rampage on to the 'Sous Hills'. The setting was a vast open space about 3 kilometres from our street and it was stacked with row upon row of liquorice roots – as high as 10–12 metres (30–40 feet).

In the summer months life was unbearable, there was no school, no money and nothing much to do. So, with a few friends from our street, off we'd go sous stealing. We crawled under ramshackle fences and climbed over monstrously high rocks in order to get to the sous hills. Silently, and with some trepidation, we collected as many of the liquorice roots as we could carry, stuffing them into our pockets and inside our shirts. Then we made for home. Things were not always so easy and occasionally one or two of us got caught. There was a little telling off, a lot of shouting, some threats and then we were sent home.

Sous, you see, was a must in the heat of the summer. It is

basically liquorice mixed with water and drunk ice cold. Nowadays I purchase my liquorice roots which are sold in most good health food and herb shops. You can buy either the root, 7·5–10 cm (3–4 in) long, or the powdered version.

Throughout southern Turkey, Syria and Lebanon sous is sold by street vendors in beautifully decorated brass containers, calling out loud 'sous, sous ya! Sous bouza' – cold sous. I have to date not found an alternative to this simple drink; certainly none of the Western concoctions (coke, lemonade, etc) can ever match the delightful and, I hasten to add, healthful glass of sous.

  6–10 liquorice roots (each 7·5–10 cm [3–4 in] long) or 10
    teaspoons liquorice root powder
  1·5 litres (2½ pints) water

1 Bring about 1·5 litres (2½ pints) of water to the boil in a saucepan.
2 Crush the roots of liquorice with a hammer.
3 Add the crushed roots (or the powder) to the water.
4 After 2–3 minutes remove the pan from the heat.
5 Allow to cool.
6 Using a strainer, or muslin bag, strain the liquid into a jug.
7 Refrigerate the juice and then serve with ice cubes.

CHAY-BI-YANASOUN
Aniseed tea

The Arabs are not great tea drinkers. They may partake in the winter months, but even then it is never with milk. Instead it is usually mixed with a herb or spice of some kind, eg cinnamon, mint, rose geranium, cloves or anis. Anis has a particular 'oriental' flavour about it, which is why it appears in so many of their recipes as well as drinks. Flavoured tea is traditionally recommended to the sick and weak as a cure for all imaginable maladies – not forgetting infertility. As the Arabs say: 'Look at those Hindis. There are so many of them. I tell you brother, it is the rice and the Chay that makes their women so bountiful.'

For each person use the following quantities:

1 teaspoon tea
$\frac{1}{2}$ teaspoon aniseed or aniseed powder
Sugar to taste

1 Make the tea in the ordinary way.
2 Add the aniseed, stir and leave for a few minutes.
3 Serve.

A DRINKING SONG

Now in Time's good tiding come;
Raise thy hopes, so long in tomb,
To the music of the strings
And good comrades' clamourings.

Call the wine, to flow again
Joyous in each joyful vein;
Bid it mingle with the heart,
Banishing all sorrows smart . . .

Pour upon the wounded soul
Healing draughts, to make it whole;
Eden's vine thy parent is,
Thou art mother of all bliss . . .

Drink, my comrade, drink with cheer
For the joy that thou art clear
Of this load of grief and care
Thy poor brother has to bear.

Patience; bear with me my brave,
If a while I seem to wave;
Thou art drunk but simply; I
Twice intoxicated lie!

Abbas Mahmud-el-Aggad,
Egyptian poet

KAHWAH
Arab coffee

> In the crowded distant coffee-house one night,
> When my tired eyes had in sight
> Faces, and hands, and legs, and light,
> While the clock scoffed at the shouts of the strong
> And struck . . .
> I heard the shadow of a song,
> The ghost of a song.
>
> From 'An ancient song' by Badr Shakir-al-Sayab, poet

Coffee is the drink of the Arabs. The drinking of it spread from the Yemen (where the plant had been introduced from Ethiopia) to Central Arabia. With the advent of the Arab tribes it penetrated Egypt, Iraq and Armenia and, via the latter, Byzantium. With the fall of the Byzantine Empire the Mongolian Turks – who were a tea-drinking people – adopted the habit of roasting and drinking coffee and so, in brief, was created the well-known Turkish coffee.

However, coffee is the drink of the Arabs and I can do no more than quote from that great writer C. M. Doughty and his masterpiece *Arabia Deserta*.

In every coffee-sheykh's tent, there is a new fire blown in the hearth, and he sets on his coffee pots; then snatching a coal in his fingers, he will lay it in his tobacco pipe. The few coffee-beans received from his housewife are roasted and brayed; as all is boiling, he sets out the little cups, 'fenjeyn' . . . When, with a pleasant gallantry, he has unbuckled his 'gutia' or cup-box, we see the nomad has not above three or four fenjeyns, wrapt in a rusty clout, with which he scours them busily, as if this should make his cups clean. The roasted beans are pounded amongst Arabs with a magnanimous rattle – and (as all their labour) rhythmical – in brass of the town, or an old wooden mortar, gaily studded with nails, the work of some nomad smith. The water bubbling in the small dellal, he casts in his fine coffee powder, 'el-bunn' and withdraws the pot to simmer a moment. From a knot in his kerchief he takes then a head of cloves, a piece of cinnamon or other spice, 'bahar' and braying these, he casts their dust in after. Soon he pours out some hot drops to essay his coffee; if the taste be to his liking, making dexterously a nest of all the cups in his hand, with pleasant chattering, he is ready to pour out for the company, and begins upon his right hand; and first, if such be present, to any considerable sheykh and principal persons. The 'fenjehn kahwa' is but four sips: to fill it up to a guest, as in the northern towns, were among Beduins an injury, and of such bitter meaning, 'this drink thou and depart' . . . Some man that receives the fenjeyn in his turn, will not drink yet – he proffers it to one sitting in order under him, as to the more honourable: but the other putting off with his hand will answer 'ebbeden', 'nay, it shall never be, by Ullah! but do thou drink!' Thus licensed, the humble man is dispatched in three sips, and hands up his empty fenjeyn.

Arab coffee is drunk without milk or sugar. Other flavourings include saffron, rosewater and cardamon.

The quantities below are for 1 person so you can increase the proportions accordingly.
The amount of sugar depends on personal taste, but the usual quantity is 1 teaspoon per person – called 'mazbout' in Arabic.

> 1 teaspoon sugar
> 1 coffee cup water
> 1 teaspoon coffee – when buying the coffee remember to ask for 'Turkish' coffee beans and make sure they are fresh and 100 per cent pulverized.

1 Mix the sugar and water together in the jaswah and bring to the boil, stirring until the sugar has dissolved.
2 Add the coffee, stir well and bring to the boil.
3 As the cofffee froths up remove the jaswah from the heat and allow the froth to subside.
4 Return the jaswah to the heat until the froth reaches the brim.
5 Remove once again.
6 Repeat this process 2 more times.

7 Remove from the heat and pour into the coffee cup.
8 Do not add more sugar and do not stir or you will disturb the sediments at the bottom of the cup.

ASAL-OU-KOUSBARAH
Coriander honey

'Come into my garden and I will give you honey and coriander' – traditional Bedouin folk song.

As the Arabs are not allowed to drink wines, beers etc because of the rules of their religion, they have, over the centuries, evolved many non-alcoholic beverages. Most are very tasty and nourishing. Some, to Western palates, are fascinating although there are a few, I am sure, which are unpalatable.

Asal-ou-kousbarah is a sweet and highly aromatic drink beloved of the Palestinians and Jordanians and known throughout most of the rest of the Arab world. It can be drunk hot or cold. The hot version is preferable on a winter's night and it is highly recommended for colds and sore throats.

For each cup of coriander honey you need:

1 cup water
2 teaspoons honey, or more depending on taste
$\frac{1}{2}$ teaspoon ground coriander

1 Warm the water in a pan.
2 Dissolve the honey in it by stirring for a minute or two.
3 Add the coriander and stir well.
4 Serve warm or cold.

AYTAN or AYRAN
Yogourt drink

This is, perhaps, the best known and most popular drink of the Middle Eastern people, beloved by the Turks, Armenians, Iranians, Arabs and the countless other nationalities of the region. It is a simple, healthful and deliciously refreshing drink that is especially popular in Syria and northern Iraq where it is sold in richly ornamented containers by street vendors. It is the ideal drink with an Arab meal.

For each cup of Aytan allow:

$\frac{1}{2}$ cup yogourt
$\frac{1}{2}$ cup water
Pinch salt
Pinch dried crushed mint

1 In a large bowl beat the yogourt until smooth.
2 Add the water and continue to beat.
3 Add the salt and mint.
4 Refrigerate for at least 1 hour.
5 Serve with ice cubes.

HALEEB-EL-LOZ
Almond milk

> As in their sea green shell the pearls
> In triple green we hide, shy girls.
> We care to pass the green of youth
> In hall berks bitter and uncouth,
> Until the waking comes and we
> Wanton white hearts from out our tree.

This is a beautiful drink made from the milk of almonds. It is popular throughout Lebanon, Palestine, Jordan and southern Syria. Almonds are abundant in the orchards of these regions and are used a great deal by the Arabs as an ingredient in their cooking.

225 g (½ lb) ground almonds
900 ml (1½ pints) water
675 g (1½ lb) sugar
2 tablespoons orange blossom water or rosewater

1 Put the ground almonds into a muslin cloth or bag and fasten securely.
2 Place the bag in a large bowl with the water for about 1–1½ hours, occasionally rubbing and squeezing the bag. Thus the almond milk will be released and the water in the bowl will turn milky.
3 Finally, squeeze the bag tightly to extract any remaining milk.
4 Pour the almond milk into a large saucepan.
5 Add the sugar and bring slowly to the boil, stirring constantly, until the sugar dissolves.
6 Just before removing the pan from the heat stir in the orange blossom water or rosewater.
7 Pour the almond milk into a jug and place in the refrigerator to chill.
8 Serve diluted to taste with ice cold water or ice cubes.

SAHLAB
A milk and resin drink

'The fly knows the face of the milk seller' – Arab saying.

Sahlab is a resin found in certain parts of the Middle East. It is obtained from the dried tubers of the plant Orchis hircina (*Satyricum hircinum*) or, as it is known in Arabic – Khussa el Kalb-Sahlab.

This delightful winter drink is made with milk and chopped pistachio nuts. Sahlab can be purchased from some Greek or Middle Eastern stores. However, it is expensive and not always obtainable. A cheaper but, I hasten to add, a non-authentic method is to use cornflour instead of sahlab.

This is often passed off as sahlab – sahlab soukhon – but in reality it is cinnamon cornflour. I suggest that if you cannot find sahlab you don't waste your time and effort using a substitute.

600 ml (1 pint) milk
1 teaspoon sahlab
2 teaspoons very finely chopped pistachio nuts or a mixture of almonds and walnuts
Pinch cinnamon powder

1 Heat the milk in a saucepan.
2 Add the sahlab, stirring all the time.
3 Lower the heat and continue cooking for about 15 minutes. By now the sahlab should be thick.
4 Pour into small dessert cups.
5 Sprinkle with the nuts and cinnamon.

Glossary

ALLSPICE: One of the most important spices used by Middle Eastern cooks. Previous to its introduction from the New World a mixture of nutmeg, cloves and cinnamon was used.

ARAK: Also known as Raki, Ouzo and Oughi is the Middle Eastern drink made usually from grape juice, but can also be prepared from dates (in Iraq) or figs (by Turks and Kurds).

BURGHUL: This is hulled wheat which is steamed until partly cooked, dried and then ground into 3 grades –
    Large – used for pilavs and stuffings
    Medium – for fillings
    Fine – for kibbehs and salads
It is not much used by the Arabs except those living on the Mediterranean coastline.
Sold in most Indian and Middle Eastern shops.

FENUGREEK: Native to the Mediterranean and most popular in Yemeni cooking. The small oval leaves are used in vegetable stews and the powdered form is used in sauces.
Can be bought in seed or powdered form.

FETA CHEESE: A popular Middle Eastern cheese that has a soft crumbly texture and is normally made from goat or ewe's milk.
Can be bought from most continental shops – otherwise substitute cottage cheese.

GHEE: (*Samna or clarified butter*).
This is pure butter fat which can be heated to high tempera-

tures without burning. Superior to ordinary butter and has a fragrance of its own.
Used in pastries, cakes, pilavs and cooking in general.

KAYMAK: (*Eishta*).

A thick cream which can literally be cut with a knife. Usually made from buffalo or cow's milk at home.
The nearest substitute is thick clotted cream.

POMEGRANATE SYRUP: (*Dibs ruman*).

Concentrated juice of the pomegranate fruit which can be found in some Middle Eastern shops.
I suggest you make your own –

    8 large, ripe pomegranates
    6 oz sugar

1 Remove the skin of the pomegranates with a sharp knife.
2 Remove the seeds from their hives by tightly squeezing the segments of the fruit in your palm.
3 Now, unless you have a fruit juicing machine, place a handful of the seeds at a time in a muslin bag and squeeze the juice out into a bowl.
4 Pour the juice into a small saucepan and heat through.
5 Add the sugar and bring slowly to the boil, stirring all the time until the sugar dissolves.
6 Lower the heat and simmer for 15–20 minutes or until the mixture thickens to a syrup.
7 Remove from the heat, leave to cool and then store in a glass jar to use as required.

ROSEWATER: (*ma'el ward*).

Used to flavour puddings, desserts and savouries it is distilled from rose petals.
Can be purchased from most continental shops as well as many chemists.

Used sparingly in drops rather than (unless suggested) spoon measures.

SUMAK: The dried crushed berries of a species of the sumak tree. It has a sour, lemony taste.
Little used in Arab cooking in general save those from northern Syria and northern Iraq.
Can be bought from some Middle Eastern stores. Ask for 'Armenian sumak'.

TAHINI: A nutty-flavoured paste made from toasted and crushed sesame seeds.
Tahini separates if it has stood for some time and so always stir before using.
Can be purchased in all Indian and Middle Eastern stores.

TURMERIC: 'The poor man's saffron is much used in Iraq and the Gulf States.
A plant of the ginger family it has a slightly bitter, resinous flavour and is yellow in colour.

This index contains the recipe titles in English; the Arabic titles appear in the Contents list at the beginning of each section of the book.

Index

International cookery books available in Panther Books

Elizabeth Cass		
Spanish Cooking	£1.25	☐
Arto der Haroutunian		
Complete Arab Cookery	£1.50	☐
Robin Howe		
Greek Cooking	£1.95	☐
German Cooking	£1.95	☐
Italian Cooking	£1.95	☐
Kenneth Lo		
Cooking and Eating the Chinese Way	£1.50	☐
The Wok Cookbook	£1.50	☐
F Marian McNeil		
The Scots Kitchen	£1.95	☐
The Scots Cellar	£1.95	☐
David Scott		
The Japanese Cookbook	£1.95	☐
E P Veerasawmy		
Indian Cookery	£1.50	☐

To order direct from the publisher just tick the titles you want
and fill in the order form.   HB581

Cooking for good health books now available in Panther Books

Ursula Gruniger
Cooking with Fruit   50p ☐

Sheila Howarth
Grow, Freeze and Cook   £1.50 ☐

Kenneth Lo
Cooking and Eating the Chinese Way   £1.50 ☐
The Wok Cookbook   £1.50 ☐

L D Michaels
The Complete Book of Pressure Cooking   £1.95 ☐

Franny Singer
The Slow Crock Cookbook   £1.95 ☐

Janet Walker
Vegetarian Cookery   £1.50 ☐

Beryl Wood
Let's Preserve It   £1.50 ☐

Gretel Beer and Paula Davies
The Diabetic Gourmet   75p ☐

David Scott
The Japanese Cookbook   £1.95 ☐

Marika Hanbury Tenison
Cooking with Vegetables   £1.95 ☐

Pamela Westland
Bean Feast   £1.95 ☐
High-Fibre Vegetarian Cookery   £1.95 ☐
The Complete Grill Cookbook   £1.50 ☐

To order direct from the publisher just tick the titles you want
and fill in the order form.   **HB381**

Cookery handbooks now available in Panther Books

L D Michaels
The Complete Book of Pressure Cooking £1.95 ☐

Cecilia Norman
Pancakes & Pizzas 95p ☐
Microwave Cookery Course £1.95 ☐
The Pie and Pastry Cookbook £2.50 ☐
Barbecue Cookery £1.50 ☐

Franny Singer
The Slow Crock Cookbook £1.50 ☐

Janet Walker
Vegetarian Cookery £1.50 ☐

Pamela Westland
Bean Feast £1.95 ☐
The Everyday Gourmet 75p ☐
The Complete Grill Cookbook £1.50 ☐
High-Fibre Vegetarian Cookery £1.95 ☐

Marika Hanbury Tenison
Deep-Freeze Cookery £1.95 ☐
Cooking with Vegetables £1.95 ☐

Sheila Howarth
Grow, Freeze and Cook £1.50 ☐

Jennifer Stone
The Alcoholic Cookbook £1.25 ☐

Beryl Wood
Let's Preserve It £1.50 ☐

Barbara Griggs
Baby's Cookbook £1.50 ☐

To order direct from the publisher just tick the titles you want
and fill in the order form. **HB681**

All these books are available at your local bookshop or newsagent, or can be ordered direct from the publisher.